THE KEY TO THE
BLESSING

Ambassador Crystal Wyatt

ELOHAI
INTERNATIONAL
PUBLISHING & MEDIA

Published by ELOHAI International Publishing & Media:

P.O. Box 64402

Virginia Beach, VA 23467

elohaipublishing.com

For inquiries or to request bulk copies, e-mail hello@elohaiintl.com.

ISBN: 978-1-953535-14-6

Printed in the United States of America

This book is dedicated to my Heavenly Father (God) who gave me this book to write and joy when it was finished. Thank you Lord for your words.

I also want to dedicate this book to my husband who is an obedient listener, who supports me during my walk of obedience to Christ.

Acknowledgements

I want to thank ELOHAI International Publishing & Media for bringing it all together for me. I especially want to thank Natasha T. Brown, she is a true communicator for Christ. I was very amazed at how she knew how to edit without taking my voice away. I appreciate her diligence, listening, and training. She is a real woman of God and a person I admire.

Thank you Dr. Gwendolyn Gonzalez who has the ear to hear from the Lord. I thank you Gwen for your direction and guidance through the Holy Spirit. This book was placed in your hands first through the command of the Lord saying, "Give it to her." I obeyed and now look at what our Heavenly Father has done.

Contents

Introduction

We as believers have been given faith to uphold, stand, believe, be faithful, and remain steadfast to God's Word. The word of the Lord says, "The just shall live by faith." Faith is living out God's Word in obedience, which in return brings the desired outcome of the blessing. The key to the blessing opens the door to what God wants to give to those who receive and respond to His Word. This key is not separate from the blessing; it is ultimately attached to it. It is very important to have this key when seeking the blessing of the Lord. Without it no one can open the door. This key requires responsibility, duty, action, and listening. What is the key you might ask? The key is obedience: listening with the intent to respond through action. We all want the blessings of God; however, we have to remember God requires obedience. This is the key that unlocks God's blessings, שמע - Shama "hear and obey."

CHAPTER ONE
ABRAHAM AND OBEDIENCE

שמע

Genesis 26:1-3 says, "And there was a famine in the land, beside the first famine that was in the days of Abraham. And Isaac went unto Abimelech, king of the Philistines unto Gerar. And the LORD appeared unto him, and said, "Go not down into Egypt; dwell in the land which I shall tell thee of: Sojourn in this land, and I will be with thee, and will bless thee, for unto thee, and unto thy <u>seed</u>, I will give all these countries, and will perform the oath which I share unto Abraham thy father."

Here, God is telling Isaac about his father's faith of obedience and giving Isaac very important wisdom about Abraham's faith and what He promised Abraham. Let's read to see why Abraham's faith was important enough that God had to speak this to Isaac, Abraham's son. While you are reading the verses below, pay close attention to the words in bold.

Genesis 12:1-4 says:

> Now the Lord had said unto Abram, Get thee out of thy country, and from thy kindred, and from thy father's house,

unto a land that I will shew thee: And I will make of thee a great nation, and I will bless thee, and make thy name great; and thou shalt be a blessing: And I will bless them that bless thee, and curse him that curseth thee: and in thee shall all families of the earth be blessed. **So Abram departed, as the Lord had spoken unto him;** and Lot went with him: and Abram was seventy and five years old when he departed out of Haran.

Genesis 17:10 and 23 reads:

10: This is my covenant, which ye shall keep, between me and you and thy seed after thee; Every man child among you shall be circumcised.

23: **And Abraham took Ishmael his son, and all that were born in his house, and all that were bought with his money, every male among the men of Abraham's house; and circumcised the flesh of their foreskin in the selfsame day, as God had said unto him.**

Genesis 21:8-14:

The child grew and was weaned, and on the day Isaac was weaned Abraham held a great feast. But Sarah saw that the son whom Hagar the Egyptian had borne to Abraham was mocking, and she said to Abraham, "Get rid of that slave woman and her son, for that woman's son will never share in the inheritance with my son Isaac." The matter distressed Abraham greatly because it concerned his son. But God told Abraham, "Do not be so distressed about the boy and your slave woman. Listen to whatever Sarah tells you because it is through Isaac that your offspring will be reckoned. I will make the son of the slave into a nation also because he is your offspring." **Early the next morning Abraham took some food and a skin of water and gave them to Hagar. He set them on her shoulders and then sent her off with the boy.** She went on her way and wandered in the Desert of Beersheba.

Genesis 22:1-3 (KJV):

"And it came to pass after these things, that God did tempt Abraham, and said unto him, Abraham: and he said, Behold, here I am. And he said, Take now thy son, thine only son Isaac, whom thou lovest, and get thee into the land of Moriah; and offer him there for a burnt offering upon one of the mountains which I will tell thee of. **And Abraham rose up early in the morning, and saddled his ass, and took two of his young men with him, and Isaac his son, and clave the wood for the burnt offering, and rose up, and went unto the place of which God had told him.**"

Genesis 22:6-12 (KJV):

And Abraham took the wood of the burnt offering, and laid it upon Isaac his son; and he took the fire in his hand, and a knife; and they went both of them together.
And Isaac spake unto Abraham his father, and said, My father: and he said, Here am I, my son. And he said, Behold the fire and the wood: but where is the lamb for a burnt offering?
And Abraham said, My son, God will provide himself a lamb for a burnt offering: so they went both of them together.
And they came to the place which God had told him of;

and Abraham built an altar there, and laid the wood in order, and bound Isaac his son, and laid him on the altar upon the wood.

And Abraham stretched forth his hand, and took the knife to slay his son.

And the angel of the Lord called unto him out of heaven, and said, Abraham, Abraham: and he said, Here am I.

And he said, Lay not thine hand upon the lad, neither do thou any thing unto him: for now I know that thou fearest God, seeing thou hast not withheld thy son, thine only son from me.

In Abram's time, God had not given a law to His people, however He spoke to Abram both audibly and through angels to communicate His will. The words in bold tell us Abraham obeyed God's directions, rules, and teaching, he responded to what God said. The result of obedience was that God gave Abraham the promised blessing of a child, Isaac, to make his descendants as numerous as the sand, and that Israel would take possession of their enemies' land (Genesis 12:7). In addition, because of Abraham's obedience, through his seed (referring to Christ) all nations on earth will be blessed (Genesis 22:17-18). From the above scriptures, we can clearly see that Abraham obeyed God, but let's examine the actual meaning of "obedience."

CHAPTER TWO
OBEDIENCE

שמע

O bedience to God is very important; when you belong to the heavenly Father, you are His child and He really expects His children to listen and respond to what He says. Don't say that you are anointed by Christ if you don't obey His word. Jesus specifically says that, "If you love me then you will keep my commandments" (John 14:15). Obedience is the key to unlocking the blessing.

Deuteronomy 28:1 reads, "And it shall come to pass, if thou shalt hearken diligently unto the voice of the LORD thy God, to observe and to do all his commandments which I command thee this day, that the LORD thy God will set thee on high above all nations of the earth" (KJV). Why do we think that Jesus is going to bless mess or bless us when we are disobedient? That's not how He works? His word specifically says, **IF**: this word is conditional, and the condition is if you do what He says by faith.

In Deuteronomy 28:1, God also says something else that is really important. He says, "If thou shalt **hearken diligently** unto the voice of the Lord thy God…" Hearken from the Ancient Hebrew Lexicon (H8085) is translated as the word "Shama" it's pronounced Shaw-mah. It means to hear, listen to obey, a careful hearing of someone or something, as well as responding appropriately in obedience or action. Diligently from the Ancient Hebrew Lexicon (H8085) also is the word "shama." It means to listen, hear, obey as well, but it tells us how we should listen; which is attentively, carefully, certainly, with consideration, intelligently (Strong's Exhaustive Concordance). In other words, shama means to hear, to obey, listen closely, or listen and to do what is said.

To receive the blessing, you have to be prepared to do the obeying part. The blessings for obedience can be found in Deuteronomy chapter 28 verses 2-14. Stop now to read this passage of scripture.

Obedience translated in Greek from the Strong's Concordance (#G5218) is hypakoē; it means to hear literally, submission to what is heard, the response of someone speaking. It's from the word origin hupakouo (#G5219) which means to obey what is heard, or acting under the authority of the one speaking, really listening to the one giving the charge (order), to hearken, obey, attentively listening, fully responsive. According to the Cambridge Dictionary, it means doing or willing to do what you have been asked or ordered to do by someone in authority. In our case, Jesus would be that authority.

God's Word is obedient to the voice of God. Isaiah 55:11 reads, "So shall my word be that goeth forth out of my mouth: it shall not return unto me void, but it shall accomplish that which I please, and it shall prosper in the thing whereto I sent it." This tells us that when God sends out His word, it does what He says and produces good results.

Isaiah 55:8-12 (NLT) reads:

"My thoughts are nothing like your thoughts," says the Lord. "And my ways are far beyond anything you could imagine. For just as the heavens are higher than the earth, so my ways are higher than your ways and my thoughts higher than your thoughts.

"The rain and snow come down from the heavens and stay on the ground to water the earth. They cause the grain to grow, producing seed for the farmer and bread for the hungry. It is the same with my word. I send it out, and it always produces fruit. It will accomplish all I want it to, and it will prosper everywhere I send it."

In other words, the obedience principle operates the same with God's Word. When He sends it out, it always obeys, and it will accomplish all that it is supposed to. It will prosper everywhere God sends it. God's Word obeys Him. Since God's Word obeys Him we should obey the word.

The writer of Psalms 119 understands obedience is key. The writer expresses that obedience glorifies God and His Word. There is really no point in getting the word if we don't obey it. It is a waste of time. The point is if you desire fruit or results, or the blessing, then make it easy on yourself and just obey. He understood the meaning of God's Word, not to just read the Bible, but to respond in action in spite of feeling, thought, or situation. I truly recommend that you read Psalms 119.

Obedience and the blessing are connected. Psalms 128:1 from the Easy-to-Read Version says, "Great blessings belong to those who fear and respect the Lord and live the way he wants." Those who are faithful to God and His Word exhibit trust in him.

That trust will bring blessings. The psalmist spoke as if the audience had obeyed faithfully and he expresses how important it is to remain faithful and obey for the sake of the blessing. This Psalm conveys that the blessing will turn others who need to change.

Obedience is important, however many fail to obey. We can't say we love Jesus and not obey him. In Matthew 22:35-37, a Pharisee, an expert of the law, tried to test Jesus and asked him, "Which is the greatest commandment of the law and Jesus replied to him and said, "Thou shalt love the Lord thy God with all thy heart, and with all thy soul, and with all thy mind. This is the first and greatest commandment. And the second is like unto it, Thou shalt love thy neighbor as thyself." Jesus was saying something they should have already known from Deuteronomy 6:5, Deuteronomy 10:12, and Leviticus 19:18. Deuteronomy 6:4-5 (NIV), the beginning of the Shema prayer reads:

> "Hear, O Israel: The LORD our God, the LORD is one. Love the Lord your God with all your heart and with all your soul and with all your strength." Deuteronomy 10:12 says "And now, Israel, what doth the Lord thy God require of thee, but to fear (respect) the LORD thy God, to walk in all His ways, and to love him, and to serve the LORD thy God with all thy heart and with all thy soul", and Leviticus 19:18 says "Thou shalt not avenge, nor bear any grudge against the children of thy people, but thou shalt love thy neighbour as thyself: I am the LORD". There is an important reason why Jesus quoted these texts to the experts of the law.

In the New Testament of the Bible, the Pharisees and Scribes knew the law but did not keep (obey) the law. See Matthew 23:2-4.

Do not be like this. It will do you no good to get the word of the Lord and fail to obey.

Deuteronomy 6:4-5 is the beginning of the Shema prayer. The people of Israel prayed these words known as the Shema in the morning and evening as a declaration of their faithfulness to God. You will understand why Jesus referenced Deuteronomy 10:12 and Deuteronomy 6:5, but first we have to understand that nothing in this world is ours. All things belong to Him and come from Him including our minds, resources, and lives. Everything we have was given by God for His honor and glory. Our job is to give honor and glory through obedience because when you really think about it, God deserves it all. Whenever we say to God, "Yes I agree with what you say and I will do it because this is my way of showing you I love you," you are acting out of obedience.

Now the first word in the Shema prayer, as translated from the Strong's Concordance (#H8085) is the word "hear." It is the word, "shama," meaning to hear intelligently with attention, with obedience, to consider, give ear, listen, respond to what you hear. Verse five says, "Love the Lord with all thy heart." This is not talking about being in an emotional state. The word "heart" is the Hebrew word Lev. It means thought, will, and emotion; loving thy Lord with all thy heart means to respond, act on, think according to His word, to respond and act on by choosing the choice God has provided for you, and respond/act based on how God feels. For example, Jesus says to have mercy on a person, and as a result, that's what you choose to do. Secondly the Shema prayer says, "Love the Lord with all thy soul." Soul translated in Hebrew is the word nephesh (H5315); it means life, whole physical being. So loving the Lord with all your soul is responding and acting on His word and instructions through your life, desires, passion, appetite, and emotion by being a blessing through your career, skills, education, business, money, lifestyle, your entire being. When you love the Lord with all your heart and your soul you use everything you have as acts or responses to God's Word for His glory. Thirdly it says, "Love the Lord with all your strength." The word "strength" does not actually mean strength as in physical strength. Consider the Hebrew word and definition for strength, which is meod (Strong's #H3966). It means muchness or abundance. In other words, these verses are instructing you to love the Lord with all your strength through responding or acting with everything you have, everything you are, every ability, every capacity—give God all you have inside, give him the best of you with excellence. So you see, obedience to God requires all of you, not parts of you.

Remember the teachers of the law and the Pharisees asked Jesus a question about the greatest commandment, and he didn't leave anything out. When he responded, "Love thy neighbor as yourself," he was quoting Leviticus 19:18. We can do this by understanding that God showed us how we should love him (through obedience) through the life of His Son, Jesus, and by doing, thinking, feeling, choosing His Word over our own. Now we have the ability to love each other or our neighbors through the reflection of His love. Neighbor means: the person near, that is in need or hurting or one who is wounded and one who can't help themselves. Love is an action word.

Don't say you love Jesus while you refuse to obey him, so likewise don't say you love your neighbor and when they are in need, you won't help them. Remember all things belong to Jesus and loving your neighbor is a reflection of how you love Jesus. In other words, your love and treatment of Jesus will show by how you love or treat others. Whenever we say, "I love Jesus and love others," we are saying to Jesus, "I will do what you say and obey because of who you are." We are telling him that He is a loving God. God gave Joshua wisdom on how to master obedience through meditating on His Word. Joshua 1:8 from the King James Version says, "This book of the law shall not depart out of thy mouth; but thou shalt meditate therein day and night, that thou mayest observe to do according to all that is written therein: for then thou shalt make thy way prosperous, and then thou shalt have good success." In other words, speak, pay attention to, think on, and do what you read from the Word of God, and eventually you will live a lifestyle of obedience to Him.

Obeying God's Word is very important to the one who believes because our heavenly father knows it will bring good results. Take for example the woman with the issue of blood for twelve years; she applied what she read in Malachi 4:2 that says, "But for you who fear My name, the sun of righteousness will rise with healing in its wings; and you will go forth and skip about like calves from the stall." She obeyed/responded to God's Word through her action. She was fully persuaded of God's Word. She demonstrated all five elements of faith: she heard (Mark 5:27), she believed (Mark 5:27b) she decided to press through the crowd in spite of the possibility of her being stoned to death, she received (Mark 5:29) by doing something, she spoke (Mark 5:28), and she acted (Mark 5:27b). The woman with the issue of blood wanted her healing so much that she pressed through the crowd of people. Women in her time were considered unclean while menstruating, and she could have been stoned to death. However she decided that no matter what she would be healed, and she fully obeyed God's Word to receive her healing. When she touched Jesus she was made whole, but after she was healed by Jesus, He felt power leave Him and He said, "Who touched me?" She came forward, and He told her, "Daughter, be of good comfort; thy faith hath made thee whole" (Matthew 9:22).

Jesus addresses her as "daughter." When reading the Scriptures, I found Jesus addressed other women as daughters as well, but why did Jesus address some this way? Galatians 3:7 (NIV) says, "Understand, then, that those who have faith are children of Abraham," and Galatians 3:9 says, "So those who rely on faith are blessed along with Abraham, the father of faith." Another verse also addresses people of faith as sons and daughters of Abraham. In Luke 19:9 Jesus told Zacchaeus, a wealthy chief of publicans, "Today salvation has come to this house, because this man, too, is a son of Abraham." See also John 8:39 and Romans 4:16. The promise that comes by faith as described in Romans 4:16 was applied to them back then and to us today for those who want the blessing of Abraham, doing the work of faith and obeying God's Word. So when we are obedient, we are called daughters and sons of God because we have obeyed or acted on the seed which was planted through God's Word, but let us not forget obedience and faith go together.

CHAPTER THREE
OBEDIENCE TO THE FAITH

שמע

Obedience to the faith is responding to what is heard, responding through faith, doing what God says, whether His Word is spoken or written. Obedience includes acting on God's will (personal choice), upholding His Word by doing what it says to do, putting God's Word into action, and believing that He will see and provide for you through the rest.

When we say, "I have faith in Jesus," we are saying: I will do what I can do to support, help, and uphold God's Word, so that the promise/blessing will manifest no matter what the situation may be. Romans 1:17 reads, "… the just shall live by Faith." Living by faith is obeying God's commands through our Lord Jesus Christ.

The Word of God says that the righteous shall live by faith. This happens through obedience because obedience is the result of God's persuasion which is actually responding to what was heard, written, or spoken. Let me start by giving you the faith hall of famers so that you can see faith in action through obedience. Hebrews 11:6 says, "And without faith, it is impossible to please God because anyone who comes to him must believe that he exists and that he rewards those who earnestly seek him" (NLT). In other words faith is needed to please God.

In verses: 4, 5 ,6, 7, 8, 9, 11, 17, 20, 21, 22, 23, 24, 27, 28, 29, 30, 31 of Hebrews chapter 11, we can read about the Biblical generals who put faith into action (through their obedience). *I've included parts of these Scriptures below so that you can get an idea of the way faith looks.* **The underlined words are the action they took which showed they obeyed faith, because faith acts! It moves! It does!**

Hebrews 11:4: "**By faith** Abel <u>offered</u> unto God a more excellent sacrifice than Cain, ..." (Genesis 4:1-10).

Hebrews 11:5: "**By faith** Enoch was <u>translated</u> (taken up, transported to heaven) that he should not see death; ..." (Genesis 5:24).

Hebrews 11:6 gives us an example of a man named Enoch. How did Enoch please God? Genesis 5:24 in the (NIV) gives us the answer, "<u>Enoch walked faithfully with God;</u>" then he was no more because God took him away." Enoch spent a lot of time with God hearing His Word which triggered him to obey God's Word through faith.

Hebrews 11:7: "**By faith** Noah, being warned of God of things not seen as yet, <u>moved</u> with fear, <u>prepared</u> an ark to the saving of his house..." (see Genesis 6:9-22)

Hebrews 11:8: "**By faith** Abraham, when he was called to go out into a place ... and <u>he went out</u>, not knowing whither he went." (see Genesis 12:1-9)

Hebrews 11:9: "**By faith** he <u>sojourned</u> in the land of promise, ..." (see Genesis 12:8, Genesis 18:9, Genesis 13:3, and Genesis 13:18)

Hebrews 11:11: "**Through faith** also Sara herself <u>received</u> strength to conceive seed and was delivered of a child ..." (see Genesis 21:2)

Hebrews 11:17: "**By faith** Abraham, when he was tried, <u>of-</u>

fered up Isaac: and he that had received the promises offered up his only begotten son, Of whom it was said, That in Isaac shall thy seed be called." (see Genesis 1-19)

Hebrews 11:20: "**By faith,** Isaac blessed Jacob and Esau concerning things to come." (See Genesis 27:27-29 for Jacob's reference.) (See Genesis 27:39-40 for Esau's reference.)

Hebrews 11:21: "**By faith** Jacob, when he was dying, blessed both the sons of Joseph…" (see Genesis 48:8-20)

Hebrews 11:22: "**By faith** Joseph, when he died, made mention of the departing of the children of Israel; and gave commandment concerning his bones." (see Genesis 50:25)

Hebrews 11:23: "**By faith** Moses, when he was born, was hid three months of his parents, because they saw he was a proper child..." (see Exodus 2:1-2)

Hebrews 11:24: "**By faith** Moses, when he was come to years, refused to be called the son of Pharaoh's daughter; Choosing rather to suffer affliction with the people of God, than to enjoy the pleasures of sin for a season; Esteeming the reproach of Christ greater riches than the treasures in Egypt: for he had respect unto the recompense of the reward." (see Exodus 2:11)

Hebrews 11:27: "**By faith** he forsook Egypt, not fearing the wrath of the king: for he endured, as seeing him who is invisible." (see Exodus 5:1; 12:40-41)

Hebrews 11:28: "**Through faith,** he kept the Passover, and the sprinkling of blood, lest he that destroyed the firstborn should touch them." (see Exodus 12:2-13)

Hebrews 11:29: "**By faith,** they passed through the Red sea as by dry land…" (see Exodus 14:5)

Hebrews 11:30: "**By faith,** the walls of Jericho fell down after they were compassed about seven days." (see Joshua 5:13-20)

Hebrew 11:31: "**By faith,** the harlot Rahab perished not with them that believed not when she had <u>received</u> the spies with peace." (see Joshua 6:23, 25)

These individuals heard God's Word and by faith they obeyed. How do we know this? If we were to read the Bible stories in parentheses, we would see that the Word of the Lord was present. Faith is with the Word of God, and all acted in obedience to the faith. Therefore, from the scriptures above we can see there is faith inside God's Word when one hears it. Again, obedience is the result of God's persuasion through His Word written or spoken. Faith automatically comes with the Word of God.

Mark 4:22 reads, "Have faith in God." The original Greek text says "Have faith from God." Faith comes out of God. He is the ultimate faithful one. In 1 Corinthians 1:9, the Bible says, "God is faithful, who has called you into fellowship with His Son, Jesus Christ our Lord." Romans 10:17 reads, "So then faith cometh by hearing, and hearing by the word of God." The two words in this verse **Cometh by** are very vital to the hearer; an example of this would be if I ask, "How did you get your paycheck?" You would say, "By working" or "through working." You receive payment because there is payment in the work. Payment is automatically connected to the work. So likewise when we hear God's Word, faith is the payment that comes through hearing and hearing God's Word which should trigger obedience.

According to this, faith comes by, with, from, and through God's Word. Now, let me give you a picture of what this "come by faith" looks like. First God's Word triggers faith. Faith triggers obedience. Obedience brings blessings, because faith without works is dead. James 2:17 (NIV) says, "Faith by itself if it is not accompanied by action, is dead." Faith without works or (obedience) is dead.

The Bible book of 1 Samuel 15:22 (KJV) says, "And Samuel said, 'Hath the LORD as great delight in burnt offerings and sacrifices, as in obeying the voice of the LORD? Behold, to obey is better than sacrifice, and to hearken than the fat of rams.'"

This tells us God wants us to obey Him rather than perform rituals. James 2:19 (NIV) reads, "You believe that there is one God. Good! Even the demons believe that-and shudder." In other words, James is saying demons believe but they are not obedient. Faith cannot mature until it is coupled with obedience.

James 2:23-24 (NIV) reads, "And the scripture was fulfilled (complete, accomplished) that says, "Abraham <u>believed</u> God, (he made the decision to act out God's Word) and it was credited to him as righteousness," and he was called God's friend. A person is considered righteous by literally doing what the Word of God says—this is an outward birth of being persuaded of God's Word.

So what did Abraham do? Well it says he believed. Believing is one of the elements of faith. Abraham put faith into action by obeying, and with that in mind that brings me to tell you, Abraham was called God's friend because he obeyed through faith (James 2:22-23).

How can we be a friend of God's? Let's read John 15:13-14 where our master Jesus Christ gives us this answer. He says, "Greater love has no one than this: to lay down one's life for one's friends" (NIV). "You are my friends **if you do what I command.**" When Jesus said first "to lay down one's life for his friend" this was more than just a surface type of friendship. It describes a friendship with deep connected roots. We can see Jesus sacrifice Himself to show how much of a friend He was to the Father; so for us it means submitting our wills and desires to His will, allowing Jesus to set our paths and lay the routes for us to take. Then we will be in harmony with Him and will be called His friends. Jesus is also saying *you are my friends if you carry out whatsoever I give or instruct you to do*—in other words, if we are obedient.

Jesus was telling His disciples that a friend is someone who is reliable, someone that will be in my corner no matter what, they are there for me, they know me, they will be loyal, dependable, supportive, and will sacrifice, and will communicate their deepest feelings and thoughts... A friend agrees with you on important things. Amos 3:3 (RSV) says, "Do two walk together unless they have made an appointment?" Appointment here means to meet at a set time and place. The idea of this word is that the two agreeing to make an appointment come together and from there set out on a journey to a place together.

Jesus said, "You are my friends if you do what I command." It is not that our obedience makes us a friend but reasonably that friendship is identified by obedience. Abraham was in exact and continual accord with God even when he did not know the end result which made him a friend of God's, and he did it all in faith.

Obedience is never easy by itself. We need faith to power us to act on God's Word. Jesus is a great example of obedience; he made a way for believers to obey the faith by obeying God the Father first, so that we can follow in His footsteps and benefit from what he did. Romans 5:19b says; "So by the obedience of one (Jesus) shall many be made righteous." Philippians 2:8 tells us what he did: "And being found in fashion as a man, he (Jesus) humbled Himself, and became obedient unto death." As an example for His believers, Jesus emptied Himself through death on the cross, where he literally died to self and totally submitted His will, thoughts, life, and feelings over to the father. He gave everything over so that His followers might become rich. Not only was He obedient unto death,

He was also obedient to death of the cross, allowing Himself to be humiliated for others.

Hebrews 5:8 reads, "Though he were a Son, yet learned he (Jesus) obedience by the things which he **suffered.**" Jesus learned obedience through allowing, permitting, or letting Himself be taken by death and hung on the cross. This level of obedience required Jesus to depend on the father intently. Matthew 26:39 says, "Going a little further, He fell face down and prayed, 'My father, if it is possible let this cup pass from me, not as I will (choose), but as you will (choose).'"

In John 10:18, Jesus says, "No one takes it from me, But I lay down of my own accord, I have authority to lay it down, and I have authority to take it up again. This charge I have received from my father" (ESV). Jesus has power and authority to lay down His life and take it up again. Jesus voluntarily gave Himself as the lamb of God. He wants us to learn obedience as well by allowing him to have complete control of the lives he has given to us. We shouldn't have a problem with this, besides they are His anyway, He knows more about us than we do, and He has a purpose for our lives.

Hebrews 5:9, states, "And being made perfect, he became the author of eternal salvation unto all them that obey him;" So in other words, Jesus became the cause of everlasting salvation to all them (ones who receive Him as Lord and Savior) that obey (listen attentively or take heed to His authority or commands). Obedience again is responding in action to what is heard. Obedience never says it's according to how you feel, if you understand, nor that you need to know the end result of what Jesus tells you to do. Jesus expects us to obey because obedience shows the characteristics of a believer's faith. We see obedience and salvation is really about a relationship with Christ. Having an intimate relationship with Christ helps the believer to obey because, just like with any close friendship, when two are close friends, they really know each other and by spending time together they grow to trust one another, especially if they have proven to be dependable. And that's where faith comes in; Jesus has shown His followers He can be trusted and since He can be trusted, we can act in faith and obey Him.

As believers, we should obey because we have been given grace through Jesus. To understand grace, we have to first go back to when it's first mentioned in the Bible. The Hebrew word for grace is "hen" (H2580) in the Hebrew Lexicon; it means the beauty of the camp, or the beauty of the camp given to others. The first time grace is mentioned is in Genesis 6:8. It says, "But Noah found grace (favor) in the eyes of the Lord." This verse gives us a picture of what grace looks like in a physical form. Here is the picture; Noah was able to obtain the power to protect His family in the ark. So the working definition of grace is to be brought into a protected place or God's camp from the outside world.

Noah was shown (grace and) favor because of His obedience. Genesis 6:9 says, "Noah was a just man (righteous), perfect (mature) and walked (lived by faith) with God." In other words, Noah obeyed God in spite of His desires. The benefit Noah received for His obedience was God's extended (grace and) favor. All this happened because Noah obeyed God through faith (by responding/ acting on what he did not see or could not see through God's Word). Ephesians 2:8 reads, "For by grace are ye saved through faith; and that not of yourselves: it is the gift of God." This verse gives us a spiritual picture of grace. The Greek word for grace translated here is "charis" (Strong's #G5485), which means kindness. Jesus decided to extend His kindness to the gentiles. Through this kindness, we can be saved through believing in the gospel of Jesus Christ. This kindness made us alive through Christ the anointed one. As adopted, engrafted believers, we should obey because we have been given grace through Jesus and we will constantly see His kindness at work in our lives. This gift of grace given by Jesus was also given to empower the believer to have the ability to trust him. Grace also empowers the believer to do the work they are called to do. Without the power that comes from grace, trusting Jesus would be impossible, and it would also be impossible to obey. Jesus fulfilled the scriptures so believers can have this grace to obey faith.

Have you ever heard the saying, "You speak so graciously"? Colossians 4:6 says something similar: "Let your conversation (speech) be always full of grace (joy, sweetness), seasoned with salt (flavor or wisdom), so that you may know how to answer everyone." We can speak this way because of Christ who has given us this gift through His Spirit and word. We know without a doubt that Jesus spoke graciously; he always knew what to say. Psalm 45:2 talks about the coming Messiah, "Thou art fairer (beautiful) than the children of men: grace (beauty) is poured into thy lips: therefore God hath blessed (praised) thee forever (eternity)." John 1:17b adds, "Grace (blessing) and truth (God's Word) came through Jesus Christ." Luke 4:22 (NIV) reads, "All spoke well of him and were amazed at the gracious words that came from his lips." When Jesus spoke, His words were beautiful and persuasive and hearing them is very important for life. In God's Word, faith comes by hearing. The Greek translation for "hearing" is translated "akoe'" (Strong's #G189), it means the sense of hearing. Therefore when you hear God's voice or hear His word, faith is attached to it. Mark 4:15 reads, "And these are they by the wayside, where the word is sown; but when they have heard, Satan cometh immediately, and take away the word that was sown in their hearts." This means the

Word of God came with faith to the people it was meant for, but they rejected it by not accepting and decided to give no thought to what was heard. As believers, we must respond through faith so that His word will bring us into righteousness.

CHAPTER FOUR
OBEDIENCE TO GOD'S WORD IS RIGHTEOUSNESS

שמע

Righteousness is a result of obedience. If you obey sin the result is death, but if you obey God, the result is righteousness. Romans 6:16 says, "Know ye not, that to whom ye yield yourselves servants to obey, His servants ye are to whom ye obey; whether of sin unto death or of obedience unto righteousness?" Romans 5:17 reads, "For if, by the trespass of the one man, death reigned through that one man, how much more will those who receive God's abundant provision of grace and of the gift of righteousness reign in life through the one man, Jesus Christ."

In 2 Corinthians 5:21, the Bible reads, "For he hath made him to be sin for us, who knew no sin; that we might be made the righteousness of God." Righteousness translated in Greek as dikaios it means "in a wide sense, keeping the commands (God's Word), innocent, faultless, guiltless, used of him (Jesus) whose way of thinking, feeling, and acting is wholly conformed to the will of God, approved of or acceptable of God, rendering to each his due" (#G1342 NAS New Testament Greek Lexicon 1999). Righteousness gives us peace with God and the ability through Jesus Christ to live a devout, upright, pure, holy life in conduct and integrity, to him, self, and others, and God's will of spiritual and natural behavior that is morally justifiable or right which can only come through Jesus Christ. It is the perfection or holiness of God's nature.

There are two aspects of righteousness. The first is the fact that believers have peace with God. The second aspect of righteousness is the believer doing what's right according to the power and guidance of the Holy Spirit. First let me speak about peace with God. Romans 5:1-2 says, <u>"Therefore, since we have been justified through faith, we have peace with God through our Lord Jesus Christ,</u> through whom we have gained access by faith into this grace in which we now stand. And we boast in the hope of the glory of God." The underlined verse is saying that because we have been declared innocent, acquitted of sin, we have peace (or oneness) with God by way of Jesus Christ, that believers are tied or joined together as one with God through Jesus. We are declared righteous because of Jesus. We are not declared righteous because of ourselves or what we did. Colossians 2:13-14 (NIV) says, "When you were dead in your sins and in the uncircumcision of your flesh, God made you alive with Christ. He forgave us all our sins, having canceled the charge of our legal indebtedness, which stood against us and condemned us; he has taken it away, nailing it to the cross."

Wow did you see that it said, **"having canceled the charge of our legal indebtedness,"** this is really good news for everyone to know. Through Jesus, all of our sins are canceled, we are declared innocent, acquitted of sin.

We have this confidence because we have peace with God because of the sacrifice of Jesus which allowed us to come near to God through faith (Hebrews 10:19-22). Now aren't you super excited that Jesus took the judgment for your sins so that you and I will not be an enemy to God? Thank you Jesus for your sacrifice! The second aspect of righteousness is the believer doing what's right according to the power and guidance of the Holy Spirit.

In Matthew 5:10 Jesus says something very interesting, "Blessed are they which are persecuted for righteousness' sake: for theirs is the kingdom of heaven." In other words, those who are persecuted for the sake of listening and obeying the spirit of God's righteousness will be blessed.

Persecuted for righteousness' sake sounds strange for Jesus to say. Why would a person who is doing what is morally right according to God's Word through Jesus Christ have this issue in their life? Well it's simple; in Romans 14:17-18 (NIV) the Bible reads, "For the kingdom of God is not a matter of eating and drinking, (Physical things) but of righteousness, peace, and joy in the Holy Spirit (Spiritual things), because anyone who serves Christ in this way is pleasing to God and receives human approval." It is about spiritual things, and most people truly don't understand the spiritual moral standard of God because they either have not been born again, have a lack of knowledge, or are just plain disobedient, and because of that, believers who are actually obedient will be attacked. The idea of righteousness is the condition of the believer; acceptable by God but not acceptable to man, because God's way is a threat to those in darkness. You see again righteousness is integrity, purity of life, rightness and correct thinking, and because of that, persecution comes, due to living life God's way.

When we receive the promise of the Holy Spirit, he is one of the many gifts we obtain from the blessing. Another gift is righteousness, and since we have righteousness in the Holy Spirit, he teaches believers how to live morally right before God, ourselves, and others.

Let's go back to Matthew 5:10 when Jesus said, "Blessed are they which are persecuted for righteousness' sake: for theirs is the kingdom of heaven." So Jesus is saying when you follow my righteous way of living according to the power that works within you; you will be harassed and troubled, but Jesus says "you will inherit the kingdom of heaven," (you will inherit all things in me). Mark 1:15 says, "And saying, the time is fulfilled, and the kingdom of God is at hand: repent ye, and believe the gospel." Jesus is commanding them to turn and change their minds from their way of thinking to obey Jesus' way of righteousness.

In the Bible, there are many instructions through Jesus to live righteous. The Sermon on the Mount in Matthew chapters five through seven gives us some ideas on how to live an ethical, righteous life.

They were learning what it takes to be true disciples of Jesus. Jesus started out with the Beatitudes in Matthew 5:1-12. Beatitudes are the blessings spoken by Jesus that refers to the condition of spiritual well-being and prosperity. These Beatitudes describe an ideal disciple's character and lifestyle and their rewards present and future. The Beatitudes also refer to a believer in Christ who is content and firm in the middle of life's hardships because of the indwelling fullness of the Spirit. After the beatitudes, Jesus said, "Ye are the salt of the earth." Jesus taught that His disciples are the ones who preserve or keep things together here on earth and if disciples lose their flavor or fail to live righteously, it would affect other people. He taught His disciples that others can see him by their righteous living and obedience. Others will choose to be disciples of Christ by the way His current disciples live. Righteousness through obedience does not only make disciples credible witnesses to Christ, but it leads to prosperous living. On the other hand, when disciples decide not to follow the commands of Jesus, they fail to be viewed as leaders who live healthy and full lives. After this, Jesus began to describe His disciples as the light of the world. He said, "So let your light shine." In other words, Jesus is saying allow the people outside of me to see the indwelling of the Holy Spirit in you, so that they can see the obedience, learn your testimony, ask you questions about your good works, and possibly begin to get to know Jesus and glorify the father as well (Matthew 5:13-16).

The purpose of The Sermon on the Mount was for Jesus to teach citizens of the kingdom how to live according to the king's word and be leaders in obedience so that others can see. Here is my outline of Matthew chapters 5-7.

★ (Matthew 5:3-12) Beatitudes how you should think, in terms of behavior.

★ (Matthew 5:13-16) Salt and light description of a kingdom believer.

★ (Matthew 5:17-48) Jesus describes Himself fulfilling the law by following obedience of righteousness and for disciples to follow him by obeying what he says.

★ (Matthew 6:1-18) Outward appearance of righteousness vs. inward appearance of Godly righteousness.

★ (Matthew 6:19-21) Storing up earthy materials vs. spiritual materials through righteousness.

★ (Matthew 6:22-23) Seeing through Jesus' perspective of righteousness or your perspective.

★ (Matthew 6:24-34) Seek His way of living and His right way of living above all else.

★ (Matthew 7:1-5) Judge rightly not hypocritically.

★ (Matthew 7:7-12) Ask righteously and do good to others.

★ (Matthew 7:13-14) Jesus' right path or the wrong way.

★ (Matthew 7:15-23) The real vs. the fake.

★ (Matthew 7:24-28) Ready vs. not ready.

Matthew chapters five through seven is Jesus' longest recorded sermon, and the writer Matthew used it to focus on Jesus' teachings on how to live ethical and righteous lives. This tells us the importance of righteous living! In doing so, Jesus says you are blessed, now and in the future. I recommend going back to read these chapters for yourself and see what a righteous life through Jesus looks like.

In Paul's letter to the Romans, we can also read instructions for righteous living as well. See Romans 12:9-21.

Jesus taught many principles on how to behave in this world because he knew evil was not far away. Being blessed by the Lord Jesus in this evil world makes you a target because of the light of Jesus on you and in you. Having this light makes you shine in darkness and His light carries responsibility.

I remember when I attended Pistis School of Ministry located in Southfield, Michigan and all our instructors said, "You are now a target." They were warning us that if we choose to live out our calling and live Godly lives in Christ Jesus, we would be troubled. The good news is that Jesus gave His strength to those in Him in this world...so we can understand and finish the course of faith. In the Bible books of Habbakuk, Romans, Galatians, and Hebrews, we are told, "The just (or righteous) shall live by faith."

In Romans 1:16-17, Paul writes, "For I am not ashamed of the gospel of Christ: for it is the power of God unto salvation to every one that believeth; to the Jew first, and also to the Greek. For therein is the righteousness of God revealed from faith to faith: as it is written, the just shall live by faith." In Galatians 3:11 Paul writes, "Now it is evident that no one is justified before God by the law, for 'The righteous shall live by faith" (ESV). The writer of Hebrews, in chapter 10:38 writes, "but <u>my righteous</u> one shall live by faith, and if he shrinks back, my soul has no pleasure in him" (ESV). In Habakkuk 2:4, the prophet writes, "Behold, his soul which is lifted up is not upright in him: but the just shall live by his faith."

In order for believers to live righteous lives, we live it through faith (persuasion of God's Word). We live by faith, or in other words, by what God feeds us through His Word, because Jesus says in Matthew 4:4, "It is written, Man shall not live by bread alone, but by every word that proceedeth out of the mouth of God." Faith in action is when believers obey and elevate God's Word above all else. In doing so we will have godly success.

THE KEY TO THE BLESSING

CHAPTER FIVE
OBEDIENCE TO GOD'S WORD WILL BRING SUCCESS

שמע

"This book of the law shall not depart out of thy mouth; but thou shalt meditate therein day and night, that thou mayest observe to do according to all that is written therein: for then thou shalt make thy way prosperous, and then thou shalt have good success."

Joshua 1:8

This scripture is a key principle to applying God's Word for God-given success. In Romans 10:17 it elaborates on this principle, "So then faith cometh by hearing, and hearing by the word of God." With this in mind, hearing is also important. In Joshua 1:8, God tells Joshua that meditating on God's Word over and over again will move him into obeying, then the benefits of obeying will push him forward and advance him in everything. The bonus is godly success that stems from receiving God's wisdom through His Word.

Through God's Word we will find good success. The Bible tells us that Jesus is the Word in John 1:1, "In the beginning was the Word (Jesus), and the Word (Jesus) was with God, and the Word (Jesus) was God." John 1:14 adds, "And the Word was made flesh, and dwelt (lived) among us, (and we beheld his glory, the glory as of the only begotten of the Father,) full of grace and truth." Revelation 19:13 says, "And he was clothed with a vesture dipped in blood: and his name is called The Word of God." The revelation that Jesus is the Word, can give us confidence that we can trust He will never fail us and will bring us to a place of success because He promises to do so. The Bible tells us, "For the word of God will never fail," (Luke 1:37 (NLT); "Heaven and earth shall pass away, but my words shall not pass away," (Matthew 24:35); and "There failed not ought of any good thing which the Lord had spoken unto the house of Israel; all came to pass" (Joshua 21:45). In Isaiah 34:16, the Bible reads, "Seek ye out of the book of the Lord, and read: no one of these shall fail, none shall want her mate: for my mouth it hath commanded, and his spirit it hath gathered them."

As you can see, there are so many verses that teach us that God's Words will never fail, and if you want good success, you should follow the word and obey it. When God was speaking to Joshua, (in Joshua 1:8) he told him to meditate on the word day and night. In God's Word there is always faith, and faith in action is obedience. Faith comes by hearing and receiving God's Word. Back to Joshua 1:8 the word **meditate** translated from the Greek definition in the NAS Exhaustive Concordance of 1897, means to growl, moan, utter, or speak consistently. If we keep meditating on God's Word, faith will come and faith will move into obedience.
Mark 4:14-20 reads:

> "The sower soweth the word. And these are they by the wayside, where the word is sown; but when they have heard, Satan cometh immediately, and taketh away the word that was sown in their hearts. And these are they likewise which are sown on stony ground; who, when they have heard the word, immediate-

ly receive it with gladness; And have no root in themselves, and so endure but for a time: afterward, when affliction or persecution ariseth for the word's sake, immediately they are offended. And these are they which are sown among thorns; such as hear the word, And the cares of this world, and the deceitfulness of riches, and the lusts of other things entering in, choke the word, and it becometh unfruitful. And these are they which are sown on good ground; such as hear the word, and receive it, and bring forth fruit, some thirtyfold, some sixty, and some a hundred".

Jesus gives a parable of the different types of hearers of the word. This is a key principle to good success. Verse fifteen says, "And these are they by the way-side, where the word is sown; but when they heard, Satan cometh immediately and taketh away the word that was sown in their hearts, (these are one time hearers)." Verses sixteen and seventeen describe those that heard the word but have no root, so they endure but for a time, but when they experience affliction or persecution due to the Word of God, they are offended. These are people who heard (past tense, one time hearers) who heard so that they could feel good at that moment. These are also glad hearers who don't have anything to anchor them in the word. Verses eighteen and nineteen discuss the hearers who receive the word yet the cares of this world, deceitfulness of riches, and lusts of other things choke the word and it does not produce fruit. These people hear the word over and over, but worry comes and chokes the word out of them because they stop hearing and obeying it. Worry takes over these people. They are distracted hearers. Verse twenty describes active hearers who receive, accept, and act on the Word of God. Have you ever heard the saying, "If you want something, go get it?" Well these last hearers want something and are not going to let any situation or circumstance stop them from receiving the results that the word is designed to produce. Jesus refers to these people as good ground (for receiving the word). This is ground that has been worked on. They work His word by taking what He gave to them, do what He said, and as a result, produce fruit, some thirty-fold, some sixty, and some one hundredfold. This sounds like good Godly success.

Let's go back to Joshua 1:8. First we read, "This book of the Law" (God's Word). The next word is "meditate," which is in the middle after God's Word (this is faith), and last we see the words "observe-to-do," which means (seeing that you obey), then he says, "you will make your way prosperous and then you will have good success." The words "prosperous" and "good success" are very important words here. If we break down the word prosperous we will have two words; which are PROSPER, the root, and the stem OUS. Prosper in Hebrew means to rush, to push forward, to pass through, advance, and thrive. The suffix "ous" from Merriam-Webster dictionary means possessing, full of, abounding in. Success in this verse means to be wise, having understanding, to have insight. Given these instructions we can read Joshua 1:8 like this: God's written word should not depart from your mouth, but you should read, growl, moan, utter, speak, seek to hear day and night so that you can see and obey in action all that is written, then you will push forward, advance and thrive; then you will act with Godly wisdom." Good success is being obedient to God's Word because God's wisdom will always advance you and His Word will never fail—it will bring good success through love.

CHAPTER SIX
LOVE & OBEDIENCE

שמע

The blessing of God is open for everyone. God made it very easy to receive, we simply have to follow the instructions. Consider the following scriptures:

1 John 2:5 (NLT)
"But those who obey God's Word truly show how completely they love him. That is how we know we are living in him."

1 John 4:8
"Whoever does not love does not know God, because God is love."

The important word in the second verse is the word KNOW; the Greek word for know is ginosko: it means to learn, come to know, knowledge of, to understand, to be intimate with, acquainted. So there is a prerequisite to love in obedience and it is knowing God in a deep relational way by being one spirit with Jesus. Those who are not acting out God's Word really do not know Him because God is the feast of love, the creator of love. In turn we can trust and obey His instructions on how to love through obedience.

Here is a breakdown of these words: "God" is translated in the Greek from Strong's #G2316 as Theos: which means the Creator and owner of all things, supreme being who owns and sustains all things. "Is" is translated in Greek as eimi from Strong's #G1510, the meaning is I am, I exist, to be, am, is, will be, to be present. "Love" is translated in Greek as agape from Strong's #G26 which means brotherly love, affection, good will, benevolence, love feast, divine. We can translate and say it in Greek like this: Theos eimi agape; God is love. There are four Greek words for love in the Bible, but I am going to focus on one of these words, "agape," and its action. Agape it is a noun, agape is the divine characteristic of God's nature: basically who he is (Strong's #G26). Agapao is a verb which means to welcome, to entertain, to be fond of, to love dearly (Strong's #G25). Agapeo comes from the Greek word phileo: it means to love, to treat affectionately or kindly, to welcome, befriend to be fond of doing. (Strong's #5384) So to make these words simple Agape is God and Agapeo is the action, response, or expression that tells us how God loves and how to love. Let's read a few scriptures about these two words.

Matthew 22:37 (NIV)

Jesus replied: "<u>Love</u> the Lord your God with all your heart and with all your soul and with all your mind." (The word "love" here is agapeo.)

Matthew 22:39 (NIV)

"And the second is like it: '<u>Love</u> your neighbor as your-self." (Love here is also agapeo.)

John 14:15 (NIV)

If you <u>love</u> me, keep my commands." (Love here is agapeo it comes from the Greek word phileo. It means to be a friend, to be fond of, to welcome, to entertain. The second word is keep, keep is tereo it comes from a Greek word theoreo that means to look upon, view attentively, contemplate, to learn by looking, look closely at, to see with the mind to perceive, to know, become acquainted with by experience, to look to, to stare at.)

In other words, Jesus is saying *if you are my friend think about what I say to you and learn from it through obedience.*

John 13:34 (NIV)
"A new command I give you: <u>Love</u> one another. As I have <u>loved</u> you, so you must <u>love</u> one another." (Love in both instances is agapeo.)

1 John 5:3 (KJV)
"For this is the <u>love</u> of God, that we keep his commands: And his commands are not a burden." (Love in this scripture is agape.)

Luke 11:42 (NIV)
"Woe to you Pharisees, because you give God a tenth of your mint, rue and all other kinds of garden herbs, but you neglect justice and the <u>love</u> of God. You should have practiced the latter without leaving the former." (The word love here is agape.)

These verses give us an understanding that love comes from God. God gives love to believers to empower them to have the ability to act out what was given to them through the seed of the word.

John 13:34 reads, "A new commandment I give unto you, That ye love one another; as I have loved you, that ye also love one another." Here is a break- down of this verse.

1. A new commandment I give you, love one another.

- Commandment: from Strong's #1785 is defined as an injunction, that is, an authoritative prescription.
- Give: from Thayer's Greek-English Lexicon means to give something to someone, of one's own accord to give one something, to his advantage, to bestow a gift. For example: as a nurse, a doctor gives me an order or command and it is my responsibility to deliver, hand out, operate, or oversee what was given to me. So likewise, God gave love so that we can offer it to one another.

2. As I have loved you… Have loved is past tense. This shows that love started from Him. Jesus showed love by action: through teaching, by revelation, through challenges, through instruction, by healing, through forgiving, by mercy, by compassion, through keeping His father's commands.

3. That you also love one another: Jesus is saying *I have shown you this so I can be your example of how to truly love.*

There is a connection between love and obedience; Jesus says, "If you love me keep my commandments." The Holy Spirit connects the two. Follow me so you can understand the connection.

Exodus 19:5-6 reads, "Now, therefore, if ye will obey my voice indeed, and keep my covenant, then ye shall be a peculiar treasure unto me above all people: for all the earth is mine: And ye shall be unto me a kingdom of priests and a holy nation. These are the words which thou shalt speak unto the children of Israel." There are four things that stand out in these verses:

1. If ye will obey my voice indeed
2. Peculiar treasure
3. A kingdom of priests, and
4. A holy nation.

First, it's interesting that God told Moses, "say to the house of Jacob, and tell the children of Israel; 'If ye will obey my voice…'" Now remember the people could not hear God's voice unless it was through a priest, king, or prophet.

Second, we should note that God said, the people of Israel shall be a peculiar treasure. The word peculiar does not mean different or weird or strange; here it means ownership or possession. God is saying *I will make you my own special people.*

It's interesting that God said "they will be a kingdom of priests and a holy nation." Now how do you expect God to do all this? Well remember he told Israel, "if ye will obey my voice indeed…" God's plan all along was to set them apart for service for Him and to guide them to listen and obey His voice.

Exodus 19:16 describes how the people of Israel heard God's voice. "On the morning of the third day there was thunder and lightning, with a thick cloud over the mountain, and a very loud trumpet blast. Everyone in the camp trembled." Prior to, Moses had to prepare the people to hear the voice of God, then God spoke to the people and gave the commands. Exodus 20:1-17 are God's commandments, which taught the Israelites how to love God through action, not of their own works, but by obeying God's loving word and through response. The first part of these commandments (Exodus 20:2-10) are instructions on how to love God and the second part of (Exodus 20:12-17) are instructions on how to love their neighbors/others. These two sections of commandments are connected to each other by love. The gist of these sections are if you love God, you love your neighbor, and if you love your neighbor, then you are loving God, and the way you love God and your neighbor is through acting out what is written or spoken from the Word of God. Exodus 20:20 reads, "And Moses said unto the people, Fear not: for God is come to prove you, and that his fear may be before your faces, that ye sin not." In this verse there's a lot of information that deals with obedience. Moses said "that his fear may be before your faces." More understanding of this verse can be found in John 4:24 which states that God is Spirit: and they that worship him must worship him in spirit and truth. "God is Spirit" means that God is the sustainer of all life, yet He cannot be seen with natural eyes. We are to worship (or respect/bow down) to him with our lives (spirit) through obeying His Word (truth). Now stay with me, because I am going somewhere with this. When Moses said, "God's fear may be before you." He was saying the fear of God is His very presence and with this presence, His Spirit is with you. My question is *who can stand in His presence?* The answer is no one, everyone has to bow, and do what's right. Psalm 34:11 reads, "Come, my children, listen to me; I will teach you **the fear of the Lord.**" In other words He is saying I will teach you how to respect and obey. I will teach you how to be in my presence and how to honor me.

When the children of Israel were in the presence of God, the Spirit of God gave them His Word to teach them how not to sin against Him. Proverbs 1:7 says, "The fear of the Lord is the beginning of knowledge, but fools despise wisdom and instruction." In other words, being in God's presence is the beginning place to learn how to apply the knowledge given by Him. Psalms 34:13-14 define fear of the Lord as keeping your tongue from evil, your lips from speaking deceit, departing from evil, doing good, seeking peace, and pursuing it."

The fear of the Lord (or being/living in the presence of the Lord) is living in obedience to Him and His ways. Let's take another look at Exodus 20:20: Moses told the people, "Do not be afraid. God has come <u>to test</u> you, <u>so that the fear of God will be with you</u> to <u>keep you from sinning.</u>" Exodus 20:20 is the reason why God gave the children of Israel the commandments, you can find the commandments in Exodus 20:1-17.

God testing them would be like a teacher giving the students a test at the end of the week after teaching a lesson and giving them an assignment based on that lesson. However the Israelites should not be in torment because all the answers are given to them freely with love without burden.

So here is the breakdown of Exodus 20:20 for better understanding; Moses says, "Don't be afraid God is come to prove you." In other words, he told them that they would be tested so that God's fear (His presence) would keep them. It's like God was giving them constructive criticism so that they would not sin. Sin translated in Hebrew is khata or chata'ah, and it means "missing the mark, an error, a mistake, or a case of missing the target or goal." With knowing the definition of sin, God gave the commandments to Israel so they could learn and act out His way to obey Him through love, by showing their love through action, and so that they would not walk in error. They had the commandments (God's Word) and God's presence. They had a double dose of God, so they would not fail. Now in Exodus 19:8 they told Moses, "All that the Lord hath spoken we will do." Moses told God what they said and God said 'ok we will see.' Here is the thing, true love is action, not just lip service!

Now let's look at John 14:15-16, and 26. Jesus said, "If you love me, keep my commandments," as He was talking to the disciples. He tells them something very important in verse sixteen, "And I will pray the Father, and he shall give you another Comforter, that he may abide (stay) with you forever; and verse twenty-six says, "But the Comforter, which is the Holy Ghost, whom the Father will send in my name, he shall teach you all things, and bring all things to your remembrance, whatsoever I have said unto you." Now if we go back and read Exodus 19:16 and John 14:15-16, and 26 we will find out from all verses they have something in common. Exodus 19:16 says; "On the morning of the third day there was thunder and lightning, with a thick cloud over the mountain, and a very loud trumpet blast." Everyone in the camp trembled; they trembled because they never heard God's voice before and this is where all of Israel can hear God's voice. Let's look at how each of these scriptures are connected.

See the Spirit of God come down so He can help them keep His covenant. You can find this in (Exodus 19:16,18). The Spirit of God came down and sat on Mount Sinai. God's Spirit came to teach them how to be like Him: a holy loving God. In John 14:15 Jesus said, "If you love me keep my commandments" and after saying this Jesus uses the word "and" at the beginning of verse sixteen. This is a conjunction that joins two sentences, so this tells us verses fifteen and sixteen are connected. He says, "**And** I will ask the Father, and He will give you another "Helper" (Comforter, Advocate, Intercessor—Counselor, Strengthener, Standby), to be with you forever.

I like how the Amplified Bible says it, "But the Helper, (Comforter, Advocate, Intercessor, Counselor, Strengthener, Standby), the Holy Spirit, whom the Father will send in My name in My place, to represent Me and act on My behalf], He will teach you all things. And He will help you remember everything that I have told you." One of the key parts of this verse is "He will help you remember everything."

In the New Testament, the Holy Spirit is living within believers, and in the Old Testament, the Holy Spirit was living outside of them. During the time of the Old Testament, God gave the children of Israel the commandments. He was with them the entire time by fire at night and cloud by day. The Holy Spirit was present back then and he is still present today to help God's people to keep His commandments of love. This is how Exodus 19:16, 18 and John 14:15-16, and 26 are connected.

Now let's go to 1 John 5:2, "By this, we know that we love the children of God when we love God, and keep his commandments." The New International Version says it this way, "This is how we know that we love the children of God: by loving God and carrying out his commands." This is very interesting. This verse is teaching us that when we love God, and keep His commandments, we are living, walking, and acting through Christ, and obeying God's commands through the power and direction of the Holy Spirit. In the book of 1 John 5:3 (NIV) we read, "In fact, this is love for God: to keep (to hold fast, to watch over) His commands." Remember back in Exodus 19:5 God said, "If you obey my voice indeed." Jesus says in John 14:26, "I will send you a comforter and he will (teach) you all things." Hearing God's voice brings us to a place of love because God is love. When we hear God's voice, love comes forth.

This is key to acting in love and keeping God's commandments. We cannot love without hearing God's Word because God's Word is all about action. There is no way we can love truly in our own natural strength. Here is something God said that I know personally. We can't love from our own natural ability. Jesus tells us to love our enemies in Matthew 5:44. An enemy is any person who has ill will towards you. We all know this is a difficult and frustrating thing to do, however when people hurt us, we can still love them. How, do you say? The Bible says in Philippians 4:13, "I can do all things through Christ (the anointed one) which strengtheneth me." We can love through Christ's power, His strength, and His way, and we have to believe that this is possible. One of the virtues of the Holy Spirit is love and he empowers us to fulfill the love of Christ. Jesus' love empowers us to obey so that we can receive the blessing, however His love requires listening.

CHAPTER SEVEN
LISTEN AND OBEY

שמע

Listening is a life or death situation when it comes to the Word of God. It is very important for the sake of the blessing. The 1828 Merriam-Webster Dictionary defines "listen" as to pay attention to sound, to hear something with thoughtful attention, to give consideration, to be alert, or to catch an expected sound. When it comes to the things of God, listening can be very useful. Listening to the voice of God will give birth to faith which will birth obedience. In Deuteronomy 5:6-21 there is a covenant relationship between God and the children of Israel. An example of this type of covenant relationship would be like a husband and wife standing before God and taking their marriage vows. In so many words, the husband and wife are saying that they both agree they will keep the promises that they have spoken and they are agreeing to the terms by which they choose to love each other for the sake of their marriage. Likewise the vows that were given by God in Deuteronomy 5:6-21 was a covenant to clarify how the marriage (covenant) between God and His people should look. This covenant also described how that marriage would birth a beautiful arrangement. (Read Deuteronomy five in its entirety.) In Deuteronomy chapter five, there is something that gives us an understanding of listening and obeying. When we read the first verse it says, "And Moses called all Israel, and said unto them, "Hear, O Israel, the statutes and judgments which I speak in your ears this day, that you may learn them, and keep, and do them."

By the words "he called all Israel," we can gather that Moses was preaching to the children of Israel and said to them, "Hear." This word hear is not your typical (simple) audible hearing with the ear. This word translated in Hebrew is shema: it means to hear intelligently often with implication of attention and obedience. Therefore, "hear" did not just mean audibly, but to listen with the intent of understanding and responding through obedient living. Verses two and three say, "The Lord our God made a covenant with us in Horeb." The Lord made not this covenant with our fathers, but with us, even us, who are all of us here alive this day." The term "The Lord our God" means He is set apart from other gods, He is the one true God, He is Elohiym: God The Father, Son, and Holy Spirit—three as one. He is their personal God *individually* and that He has chosen them and cut them off or separated them from the rest of the nations through an agreement of His love, by redeeming them from slavery and bondage in Egypt (God gave them grace). Verse four says, "The Lord talked with you face to face in the mount out of the midst of the fire."

Moses reminded the children of Israel that God spoke to them face to face; they heard His voice for the first time, because Moses was the mediator who stood between them and the Lord. Then in verse six God basically spoke and introduced Himself and reminded them, He rescued them by His praiseworthy grace (favor) and because of this, He did not expect for them to obey because of the law which was given after the covenant, but because they could hear (shema), listen, and obey. They could listen with the intent of understanding by responding through living out His covenant words to the point of them showing how thankful they were. God did not have to, but He chose to rescue them, therefore the children of Israel should have obeyed because of the salvation that they had already received.

Let's think about this: God decided to save, rescue, and deliver His people not because they did something to deserve it, but because He is "I AM." I AM expresses who He is towards His people. It means He is the bread of Life: the sustainer for all life, (John 6:35, 41, 48, 51). He is the light of the world, which causes all things to manifest (John 8:12). He is the door to the sheep: the entrance for salvation (John 10:7, 9). He is the Good Shepherd: the good protector, feeder, and leader (John 10:11,14). He is the resurrection and the life: the redeemer and creator of all life (John 11:25). He is the way, the truth, and life: the path, reality, and eternal life giver (John 14:6). He is the true vine: the one who causes growth and gives nourishment to those who are in Him (John 15:1, 5).

Just as God wanted them to know who He is, He wants us born again believers to know as well. God wants His people to obey (respond) because He cares about their well-being. He is willing and open to show how much He loves and desires to give good and do good to His own and others who receive Him. He also cares how we treat each other. He gave the second part of the covenant so that they would understand that He is a Holy God and they should be holy as well. With all this being said, you have to be willing to understand that God is telling them that they had to listen and obey. In the four Gospels, Jesus speaks of understanding in His parables when He would say, "Who hath ears to hear, let him hear." Jesus was saying that anyone with the mind to listen and understand should obey, but it is a decision a person has to make after hearing the word of God. You can choose to obey or not to obey. It's our responsibility to use the faculty of our eyes and ears Jesus gave to us and pay attention to His word, so that the blessing that God gave will manifest in our lives. The Lord wants His followers, His children, to listen and obey Him, He commands us. Here are a few scriptures that command us to listen and obey; as you read you will see how listening is vital.

Genesis 26: 4-5 (KJV)
"And I will make thy seed to multiply as the stars of heaven, and will give unto thy seed all these countries; and in thy seed shall all the nations of the earth be blessed, Because that Abraham obeyed my voice, and kept my charge, my commandments, my statutes, and my laws."

Exodus 15:26 (NIV)
"He said, "If you listen carefully to the Lord your God and do what is right in his eyes, if you pay attention to his commands and keep all his decrees, I will not bring on you any of the diseases I brought on the Egyptians, for I am the Lord, who heals you."

Deuteronomy 13:4 (NIV)
"It is the Lord your God you must follow, and him you must revere. Keep his commands and obey him; serve him and hold fast to him."

Proverbs 4:20-21 (NIV)

"My son, <u>pay attention to</u> what I say; <u>turn your ear to my words.</u> Do not let them out of your sight, <u>keep</u> them within your heart."

Malachi 2:2 (NIV)

"'If you do not <u>listen,</u> and if you do not resolve to honor my name, says the LORD Almighty, 'I will send a curse on you, and I will curse your blessings. Yes, I have already cursed them, because you have not resolved to honor me.'"

Matthew 7:24 (KJV)

"Therefore whosoever <u>heareth</u> these sayings of mine and doeth them, I will liken him unto a wise man, which built his house upon a rock."

Luke 11:28 (NIV)

"He replied, 'Blessed rather are those who <u>hear</u> the word of God and <u>obey it.</u>'"

James 1:25 (NIV)

"But whoever looks intently into the perfect law that gives freedom, and continues in it-not forgetting what they have <u>heard,</u> <u>but doing it</u>—they will be blessed in what they do."

These are just a few verses about listening and obeying. These scriptures teach us not to just allow the word to come in, but respond to what the Spirit of God is saying. The idea of listening is not so much about just hearing, but doing what is heard. The doing part is more important to Jesus than just looking at His word and quoting it.

Here are definitions of the word **"listen"** from Strong's Hebrew and Strong's Greek translation meanings with scripture, so that you can understand listening from a Biblical perspective.

- Hebrew #238 - azan: to give ear, listen to). It is pronounced aw-zan' An example would be found in Psalms 135:17: "They have ears, but they <u>hear</u> (azan) not; neither is there any breath (word) in their mouths."
- Hebrew #8085 - shama: to hear and obey. An example would be found in Genesis 24:52: "And it came to pass that, when Abraham's servant <u>heard</u> (shama) their words, he worshipped the Lord, bowing Himself to the earth."
- Hebrew #7181 - qashab: to incline (ears), attend. This word is pronounced kaw-shab. An example would be found in Isaiah 32:3, "Then the eyes of those who see will not be blinded, And the ears of those who <u>hear</u> (qashab) will listen attentively."
- Hebrew #6279 - athar: to pray, supplicate, intercede recip-rocally, listen to prayer to intreat. This word is pronounced aw-thar. An example can be found in Isaiah 19:22: "And the Lord shall smite Egypt: he shall smite and heal it: and they shall return even to the Lord, and he shall be <u>intreated</u> (athar) of them, and shall heal them."
- Hebrew #6963 - qol: sound, voice, crackling, cry crying, growl*, listen, loudly. The pronunciation is kole. An example of this can be found in Genesis 27:22: "And Jacob went near unto Isaac his father; and he felt him, and said, "The voice (qol) is Jacob's voice, but the hands are the hands of Esau."

- Greek #1522 - eisakouo: to listen, to obey. This word is pronounced ice-ak-oo'-o. An example of this can be found in 1 Corinthians 14:21: "In the law it is written, With men of other tongues and other lips will I speak unto this people; and yet for all that will they not hear (eisakouo) me, saith the Lord."

- Greek #1874 - epakroaomai: to listen attentively. This word is pronounced ep-ak-ro-ah'-om-ahee. An example of this could be found in Acts 16:25: "And at midnight Paul and Silas prayed, and sang praises unto God: and the prisoners heard (epakroaomai) them."

- Greek #1873 - epakoúō: properly, listen appropriately, attentively "with the implication of heeding and responding to what is heard," to really listen, with suitable (attentive) hearing. Pronounced ep-ak-oo'-o. An example of this can be found in 2 Corinthians 6:2 (A Conservative Version): "he waits, I have heard (epakouo) thee in a time accepted, and in the day of salvation have I succoured thee: behold now is the accepted time; behold, now is the day of salvation."

- Greek #191 - akouo: 191 akoúō – properly, to hear (listen); (figuratively) to hear God's voice which prompts Him to birth faith within. Pronunciation is ak-oo'-o; An example of this can be found in Romans 10:17: "So then faith cometh by hearing (akouo), and hearing by the word of God."

- Greek #5219 – hupakouo: acting under the authority of the one speaking, really listening to the one giving the order. It is pronounced hoop-ak-oo'-o. An example of this can be found in Philippians 2:12: "Wherefore, my beloved, as ye have always obeyed (hupakouo), not as in my presence only, but now much more in my absence, work out your own salvation with fear and trembling."

- Greek #1582 – ekkrémamai: (from #1537 /ek, "out from and to" and #2910 kremánnymi, "to hang, hinge") properly, out from (one's own perspective) and to (the new focus), i.e. with the outcome of being totally captivated by someone's every word; "spellbound" – hanging on to each word as a listener is "suspended in rapt attention." It is pronounced ek-krem'-am-ahee. An example can be found in Luke 19:48: "And could not find what they might do: for all the people were very attentive (ekkremamai) to hear him."

- Greek #1801 - enotizomai: to receive into the ear; give ear to. It is pronounced en-o-tid'-zom-ahee. An example of this can be found in Acts 2:14: "But Peter, standing up with the eleven, lifted up his voice, and said unto them, Ye men of Judaea, and all ye that dwell at Jerusalem, be this known unto you, and hearken (enotizomai) to my words."

- Greek #202 - akroates: a hearer from akroaomai (to listen; apparently an intensive of akouo); a hearer (merely). The pronunciation is ak-ro-at-ace'. An example of this can be found in James 1:22: "But be ye doers of the word, and not hearers (akroates) only, deceiving your own selves."

- Greek #201 - akroaterion: from akroaomai (to listen) and - térion (denoting place). The pronunciation is ak-ro-at-ay-ree-on. An example of this can be found in Acts 25:23: "And on the morrow, when Agrippa was come, and Bernice, with great pomp, and was entered into the place of hearing, with (akroterion) the chief captains, and principal men of the city, at Festus' commandment Paul was brought forth."

- Greek #1251 - diakouo: hear one through, hear to the end, hear with care, hear fully. This word is pronounced is dee-ak-oo-om-ahee. An example of this can be found in Acts

23:35: "I will hear thee, said he, when thine accusers are also come. And he commanded him to be kept in Herod's judgment hall."

As you can see, listening and obeying is connected to the blessing and how can we hear if we don't have the Word of God? Now that you see and understand the concept of "listen and obey," we are now ready to discuss the blessing.

CHAPTER EIGHT
THE BLESSING

שמע

The blessing of Abraham and Definition
Genesis 12:1-3
"Now the Lord had said unto Abram, Get thee out of thy country,
and from thy kindred, and from thy father's house, unto a land that
I will shew thee: And I will make of thee a great nation, and I will
bless thee, and make thy name great; and thou shalt be a blessing:
And I will bless them that bless thee, and curse him that curseth
thee: and in thee shall all families of the earth be blessed". Here is
where God spoke the blessing to Abram but at the very end of
verse three, God says to Abram "And in thee shall all families of
the earth be blessed."

The word blessed here is speaking of the present and future
tenses. Blessed is the Hebrew word barak. it means to bend
at the knee to present a gift by giving from the palm of the
hand and to bring a gift to another while kneeling out of respect. It
also means to give or receive an inheritance (house, family, land) an
inheritance something of value from someone as a sign of the favor
someone has towards you.

What is the blessing?

The blessing is the spoken word of God to bless people physically and spiritually, the good news of God's kindness giving of His Son, the power with the indwelling Spirit of God of the coming kingdom, and salvation obtained through Christ. The blessing is granted or inherited through Jesus the Christ to the ones who believe in Him through faith. It includes gifts for both physical and spiritual life to empower and prosper believers. The blessing is the plan of salvation, the work and gift of the Holy Spirit, plus many more benefits for those who receive and believe in Jesus the Christ as Lord and Savior. In Romans 1:16, the Apostle Paul writes, "For I am not ashamed of the gospel, because it is the power of God that brings salvation to everyone who believes: first to the Jew, then to the Gentile." This verse is important because the gospel of Christ is the miracle saving power that saves all who hear and accept it. Jesus said no one comes to the father except through him. This is God's plan for salvation for all mankind, that through the Gospel of Christ (the good news about the anointed one) all people would be saved. The Apostle Paul notes that in the Old Testament God spoke through the prophets about the promise of salvation through His Son (Romans 1:1-6). Romans 1:17 tells us that the Gospel of Christ gives believers the gift of righteousness which comes from God and gives the one who believes; the position to be in right standing before God.

The blessing is a part of our spiritual inheritance. Ephesians 1:3 says, "Praise be to God and father of our Lord Jesus Christ, who has blessed us in heavenly realms with every spiritual blessing <u>in Christ.</u>" Specifically it says at the end of the verse that the blessing belongs to those "in Christ." He was referring to those in union with

Jesus the Christ. We first have to understand we have to allow God to impregnate us with His Spirit (His breath, wind, the spiritual word from His mouth) so that we can birth out the blessing. When God spoke to Abram in Genesis 12:1-3 he planted a seed. This seed came in the form of His word. God had to impregnate Abram (first with His word) so that the blessing could come fourth. Again in Ephesians 1:3, Paul says, "He has blessed us." Paul is referring to Jesus Christ. Therefore Jesus has impregnated us with His seed, which is the Holy Spirit, so that we can cultivate what was planted by our responding, acting on, or obeying what was said. This will produce the seed's intended harvest.

The blessing comes from having an intimate relationship with God. This is the connection point. Deuteronomy 28:1 says, "Now it shall come to pass if you diligently obey the voice of the Lord your God..." this tells us in order to hear to obey you have to stay close to God. You do this by living a righteous life according to His word. This will enable the blessing to rain on you. God confirmed our need to be righteous when he told Abram in Genesis 17:1, "When Abram was ninety-nine years old, the Lord appeared to Abram and said to him, "I am Almighty God; walk before Me and be blameless."

Now let's review the account of Jesus' conception from the narrative in Luke 1:26-37 (NIV):

"In the sixth month of Elizabeth's pregnancy, God sent the angel Gabriel to Nazareth, a town in Galilee, to a virgin pledged to be married to a man named Joseph, a descendant of David. The virgin's name was Mary. The angel went to her and said, "Greetings, you who are highly favored! The Lord is with you," Mary was greatly troubled at his words and wondered what kind of greeting this might be. But the angel said to her, "Do not be afraid, Mary; you have found favor with God. You will conceive and give birth to a son, and you are to call Him Jesus. He will be great and will be called the Son of the Most High. The Lord God will give him the throne of his father David, and he will reign over Jacob's descendants forever; his kingdom will never end." "How will this be," Mary asked the angel, "since I am a virgin?" The angel answered, "The Holy Spirit will come on you, and the power of the Most High will overshadow you. So the holy one to be born will be called the Son of God. Even Elizabeth, your relative is going to have a child in her old age, and she who was said to be unable to conceive is in her sixth month. For no word from God will ever fail." "I am the Lord's servant," Mary answered. "May your word to me be fulfilled." Then the angel left her."

When the angel told Mary that she would give birth to a son, notice that he simply spoke God's Word to her. He told her that no word of God's will ever fail. Mary came into agreement with the Lord's Word as sent to her through the angel Gabriel. In her response, "may your word to me be fulfilled..." she was saying may it be established, made, or created. She literally received the seed of the word.

Everything in the Old Testament was a shadow of the things to come through the seed of God that would come forth. Isaiah 9:6a reads, "For a child is born, to us a son is given." This sounds like a gift to me, which brings me to the most important point that you may have already realized. <u>Jesus is the blessing.</u> Our heavenly father said something very special to Abram in Genesis 15:5, "And he brought him forth abroad, and said, Look now toward heaven, and tell the stars, if thou be able to number them: and he said unto him, So shall thy seed be." The word seed is singular and this seed whom He was talking about was Christ. We know this to be true because Galatians 3:16 says, "The promises were spoken to Abraham and to his seed." Scripture does not say "seeds," meaning many people, but "and to your seed," meaning one person, who is Christ.

Back to Genesis 12:3c God told Abram, "All the families on earth will be blessed through him" talking about Jesus the Christ. How would this happen? It all starts with Jesus. He is the beginning of how God will give His blessing to those who have the faith of Abraham and receive His Son Jesus the Christ. Through Him—the seed, Jesus Christ, the blessing will come upon and in the nations. Those who believe and receive Him by His Spirit will also receive the blessing.

John 3:16 confirms this truth, "For God so loved the world that he <u>gave</u> his only begotten son, that whosoever believes in him should not perish but have eternal life." The word "gave" tells us what God did. Gave means to bestow, bring forth, commit, put, deliver up, give, grant, hinder, make minister, offer, set smite with the hand and strike with the palm of the hand; take, utter, yield. These are very interesting definitions that describe what God did, but many of these words also describe the actions taken by and put upon Jesus. He bestows gifts, He brings forth life. He was committed to the father. He was delivered up for our sake. He was given as a sacrifice. He granted new life. He hinders the curse. He made a new way. He was a servant and minister. He offered Himself. He possesses power. He put things back in order. He receives sinners. He set the captives free. He was smitten for our transgressions. He was stricken on the face with a palm of a hand. He suffered. He took all our sickness and diseases. He uttered or spoke God's Words, and he yielded to the

Spirit of God. Jesus is the one who took it all for the world.

Jesus was the first born of many brothers and sisters (Romans 8:29) and he comes with many gifts. Keeping in mind that Jesus is our big brother, consider that in biblical Hebrew culture the father blessed the oldest son. Therefore, since Jesus is the first born of many, all believers in Christ are His little brothers and sisters, and we are family; that means we get to partake in all that Jesus has and more. Romans 8:17 says, "We are heirs, heirs of God and joint heirs with Christ." Ephesians 1:3 adds, "We are blessed with every spiritual blessing in Christ." Colossians 1:12 adds to that, "We are partakers of the inheritance in the saints in the light." In other words, when Jesus died all that He had fell on those who are believers of Jesus Christ. It was God's will that we inherited every blessing through the death and resurrection of Christ. An example of an inheritance is when someone dies and they leave a will and the family or children receive the inheritance. Likewise, Jesus died and gave His inheritance to God's children. We partake of His divine nature (2 Peter 1:4), His holiness (Hebrews 12:10), of His Holy Spirit (Hebrews 6:4), His heavenly calling (Hebrews 3:1), His suffering (1 Peter 4:13), God's promise in Christ (Ephesians 3:6), His grace (Philippians 1:7) His fruit (2 Timothy 2:6), and His glory (1 Peter 5:1). Jesus was given every lavish gift so that He could pass them on.

Who are the families of the earth that are blessed?

Again when God spoke the blessing to Abram he said specific words, "And in thee shall all families of the earth be blessed." Who are all the families God is speaking of? Acts 3:25 says, "Ye are the children of the prophets, and of the covenant which God made with our fathers, saying unto Abraham, And in thy seed shall all the kindreds of the earth be blessed. Unto you first God having raised up His Son Jesus, sent him **to bless you,** in turning away every one of you from His iniquities." Galatians 3:14 says, "That the blessing of Abraham might come on the Gentiles through Jesus Christ; that we might receive the promise of the Spirit through faith." This means that all who were the children of the prophets; all who were under the covenant God gave to Abraham, and all gentiles who believe in Christ shall receive the blessing of Jesus and everything that Jesus has.

When God mentioned unto all families of the earth He was talking about the Hebrews (descendants of Abraham through Isaac) and the Gentiles (non-Hebrew) who receive and believe in Jesus. Genesis 22:18 says, "And in thy seed (God's Son Jesus) shall <u>all the nations</u> of the earth be blessed; because thou hast obeyed my voice." **(This refers to descendants of Abraham through Isaac and to those who are in Christ that believe and receive Him.)** Abraham obeyed God and through Abraham's lineage the Messiah will come and the blessing will come to all who believe in Him.

Genesis 12:3c says all the nations of the earth shall be blessed. Nations translated in Hebrew is the word mishpachah, which means clan, family, species, kind, circle of relatives. In the new testament Acts 3:25 says, "Ye are the children of the prophets, and of the covenant which God made with our fathers, saying unto Abraham <u>and in thy seed all the kindreds</u> (Old Testament Hebrews and New Testament Christians) of the earth be blessed. Just as Abraham was persuaded through God's Word and believed and obeyed by responding through action (and it was accounted to him as righteousness and the result was the blessing), believers under the New Testament covenant will also be counted as righteous. Galatians 3:9 confirms, "So those who rely on faith are blessed along with Abraham, the man of faith" (NIV). If you want in on the blessing take note from Abraham.

Let's go to Genesis 22:18. God told Abraham, "In thy seed," I could give definitions for all three words; however, when I began to study all three words, the Great teacher, who is the Holy Spirit gave me the definition in the simplest way. He said "in thy seed" means "with my own life." It was referring to Christ the anointed one, the one who has the blessing to give by anointing, through the touch of His hand. He is blessing those who come into the family of God, by receiving Him as Lord and Savior and thereby receive the gifts of the Holy Spirit. When God said to Abraham, "In thy seed," (Genesis 12:3, 18:18, 22:18) now don't misunderstand it. Indeed, it referred to the bloodline of Abraham, but God was not only talking about Abraham or His Son Isaac, He was referring to Jesus the Christ. Galatians 3:16 says, "Now to Abraham and his seed were the promises made. He saith not, And to seeds, as of many; but as of one, And to thy seed, <u>which is Christ.</u>" In addition, Psalm 72:17 says, "His name shall endure forever: his name shall be continued as long as the sun: <u>and men shall be blessed in him:</u> all nations shall call him blessed." Romans 1:3 adds, "Concerning his Son Jesus Christ our Lord, which was made of <u>the seed of David</u> according to the flesh."

How is God going to bestow the blessing?

Here are a few verses from the Bible stating how God will bestow the blessing.

Jeremiah 31:31-34

"I will make a new covenant with the house of Israel, and with the house of Judah: I will put my law in their inward parts, and write it in their hearts; and will be their God, and they shall be my people. I will forgive their iniquity, and I will remember their sin no more."

Jeremiah 32:39-40

"I will give them one heart, and one way, that they may fear me for ever for the good of them, and of their children after them, And I will make an everlasting covenant with them, that I will not turn away from them, to do them good; I will put my fear in their hearts, that they shall not depart from me."

Ezekiel 11:19-20

"I will give them one heart, I will put a new spirit within you; I will take the stony heart out of their flesh, and will give them a heart of flesh: That they may walk in my statutes, and keep mine ordinances, and do them: and they shall be my people, and I will be their God."

God had prophesied and promised that He would give these blessings and that He would do it according to His will, and He made good on those promises. He kept His Word.

Now let's go to the New Testament where Jesus commanded His disciples to wait for the promise.

Acts 1:4-5

"And, being assembled together with them, commanded them (the disciples) that they should not depart from Jerusalem, but wait for the promise of the Father, which, saith he, ye have heard of me. For John truly baptized with water; but ye shall be baptized with the Holy Ghost not many days hence."

In Acts 1:4, Jesus told the disciples to "wait for the promise." I'm going to give you some interesting information about this word "promise" because the definition is quite fascinating. The definition is lengthy, but stay with me. "Promise" in the Greek is epaggelia (Strong's #1860). This word means an announcement. Epaggelia comes from another Greek word epangello (Strong's #1861) which means to announce upon, to engage to do something. Epangello comes from two Greek words Epi (#G1909), which means super-imposition of (time, place, order) and the Greek word Aggelos (Strong's #G32), which means a messenger, an angel, by implication a pastor. Aggelos comes from a Greek word Aggello meaning to bring tidings. Aggello is from Ago (Strong's #G71), which means to lead, bring, drive. To sum this all up, the promise is more than an announcement; the promise is the messenger who came upon the disciples on the day of Pentecost from heaven to announce the good news of Jesus Christ and the coming in-dwelling of the Holy Spirit to lead, drive, and bring fourth power, to bring people to repentance, and to baptize by the name of Jesus Christ for the cancellation of sins, and for the receiving of the gift of the Holy Spirit.

What was the announcement? We can find it in Galatians 3:8: "And the scripture for seeing that Jesus would justify the heathen through faith preached before the gospel unto Abraham, saying, 'In thee shall all nations be blessed,' (Genesis 12:3)." It's also described in Galatians 3:14: "That the blessing of Abraham might come on the Gentiles through Jesus Christ; that we might receive the promise of the Spirit through faith." The promised blessing through Jesus Christ, received by faith is the Holy Spirit. Acts 2:33 specifically says, "Therefore having been exalted to the right hand of God, and having received from the Father the promise of the Holy Spirit, He has poured out this (blessing) which you both see and hear." There is something we must understand; Jesus is the beginning of the blessing and anyone who receives Him receives His blessing, His Holy Spirit.

The prophet Joel said "God will pour out his Spirit" (Joel 2:28), and that is what happened on the day of Pentecost: (the birthday of the living Church). This was the day that God's promise of the blessing was fulfilled. After the Spirit came upon the disciples on this day of Pentecost, the disciple Peter began to speak what the Prophet Joel said. Now after the Spirit of promise came and spoke through him and the other disciples, the people who heard the disciples speaking other languages, in their own native languages, tongues and dialects thought the disciples were drunk. Peter let them know "we are not drunk;" he explained to the people what happened. In Acts 2:17-21, Peter echoed Joel's prophecy and explained:

> And it shall come to pass in the last days, saith God, I will pour out of my Spirit (the Spirit of Jesus) upon all flesh: and your sons and your daughters shall prophesy, and your young men shall see visions, and your old men shall dream dreams, And on my servants and on my handmaidens I will pour out in those days of my Spirit; and they shall prophesy: And I will shew wonders in heaven above, and signs in the earth beneath; blood, and fire, and vapor of smoke: The sun shall be turned into darkness, and the moon into blood, before that great and notable day of the Lord come: And it shall come to pass, that whosoever shall call on the name of the Lord shall be saved (Joel 2:28-32).

Joel's prophecy included intense judgement upon the earth to come, but in the middle of the prophecy, God promised that His Spirit will be poured out for salvation, there is a condition, "That whosoever shall call on the name of the Lord shall be saved." The blessing comes through hearing and responding with action.

God said to the children of Israel in Deuteronomy 6:4a, "Hear O Israel: The LORD our God, the LORD is one." "Our God" is translated in Hebrew (Strong's #H430) as Elohiym. Elohiym is a plural noun meaning more than one persons/gods. In other words, Deuteronomy 6:4 is speaking of the triune God who is God the Father, God the Son, and God the Holy Spirit. Deuteronomy 6:4 also says, "The LORD is one." The word one translated in Hebrew (Strong's #H259) as echad: it means united, alike, alone, altogether, one and the same. The Father, Son, and Holy Spirit have different jobs, but are the same in name, aim, and purpose. They altogether saved mankind to provide the blessing to all who would hear and obey through anointed love. Anointed love means poured out to bestow through the channel of an act. Romans 5:5 says, "And hope does not put us to shame, because God's love has been poured out into our hearts through the Holy Spirit who has been given to us" (NIV). How did God do this? Romans 5:8 gives us the answer, "But God demonstrates his own love for us in this: While we were still sinners, Christ died for us" (NIV). The word demonstrates means to stand together, in union with, to line up with each other to support. The Father, Son, and the Holy Spirit altogether in union, in love glorify one another showing the world their love. Here are some verses that show us that they are one and they glorified each other.

John 10:30 (NIV)

Jesus said, "I and the Father are one."

John13:31-33 (AMP)

So when Judas had left, Jesus said, "Now is [the time] the Son of Man [to be] glorified, and God is glorified in Him; [if God is glorified in Him,] God will also glorify Him (the Son) in Himself, and will glorify Him at once." (key words in Him/ in Himself)

John 17:1-5 (NIV)

After Jesus said this, he looked toward heaven and prayed: "Father the hour has come. Glorify your Son, that your Son may glorify you. For you granted him authority over all people that he might give eternal life to all those you have given him. Now this is eternal life: that they know you, the only(one) true God, and Jesus Christ, whom you have sent."

John 16:13-15 (NIV)

"But when he, the Spirit of truth, comes, he will guide you into all the truth. He will not speak on his own; he will speak only what he hears, and he will tell you what is to come. He will glorify me because it is from me that he will receive what he will make known to you."

Matthew 28:19 (NIV)

Therefore go and make disciples of all nation, baptizing them in the name of the Father and Son and of the Holy Spirit."

As you can see, God the Father, Son, and Holy Spirit glorified one another in love and are one. Deuteronomy 6:4 says, "The LORD our God, the LORD is one," also tells us that there is only one God and He is first in the lives of Israel and also to believers. We have to respect God, hear and obey. I want to share something the Lord said to me on the morning of December 31, 2019. The Lord said, "Read Malachi 3:7. It says, 'Ever since the time of your ancestors you have turned away from my decrees and have not kept them. Return to me, and I will return to you, says the LORD Almighty'" (NIV). I learned that the word return means to turn back (Strong's #H7725). *That sounds like repentance to me...*

I said, "Lord what did these people turn from?"

He said, "Away from my decrees and have not kept them." Then the Lord had me go look at a very well-known preacher who was giving the word for the year of 2020 and the known preacher read Acts 2:14-17 (KJV). He said, "Peter, standing up with the eleven, lifted up his voice, and said unto them, Ye men of Judaea, and all ye that dwell at Jerusalem, be this known unto you, and hearten to my words: For these are not drunken, as ye suppose, seeing it is but the third hour of the day. But this is that which was spoken by the prophet Joel; And it shall come to pass in the last days, saint God, I will pour out my Spirit upon all flesh: and your sons and your daughters shall prophesy, and your young men shall see visions, and your old men shall dream dreams."

The well-known preacher said, "Now I'm gonna read it just like this, it shall come to pass in 2020. I'll pour out my Spirit upon all flesh your sons and daughters shall prophesy. Here it is! **Your young men shall see visions and your young men shall dream dreams.**" The Lord said to me the well-known preacher I had you to look at missed it. He did not say everything I told him. He left out prophesy. The Lord said, "These people who I am raising up that are going to prophesy and have visions and dreams are going to be talking to the church. The people who they are going to talk to are big well-known preachers who are shepherds over the church, the Lord said, and they are not gonna like it. The Lord said what is happening in the church is: they have gone away. They have turned away. I am getting ready to raise up those people that are going to have visions and dreams and prophesy to His people so they (the church) can repent. He said the well-known preachers are not going to like it. I have been hiding and preparing the people I am raising up." The reason why the Lord wants me to share this with you is because when the children of Israel heard "the Lord our God, the Lord is one" (Deuteronomy 6:4) they had to understand that God is the only God and He had to be the first priority in their lives. God wants us to know this same word for today. We have to respect God and obey Him and make Him priority. If you repent and call on the name of the Lord, you will be saved, He is still speaking to us today.

Now in John 7:39 Jesus said, "But this spake he (Jesus) of the Spirit, which they that believe on him should receive: for the Holy Ghost was not yet given; because that Jesus was not yet glorified." The Prophet Isaiah said, "For I will pour water upon him that is thirsty, and floods upon the dry ground: I will pour My Spirit upon thy seed, and My blessing on thy off spring" (Isaiah 44:3). Water represents life, so God would pour out of His hand, His life of the spirit to those who are deprived of spiritual life. This promise resurrected the dead and brought people back to life, back to the Father.

In Acts 2:38 the Bible reads, "Then Peter said unto them, repent, and be baptized every one of you in the name of Jesus Christ for the remission of sins, and ye shall receive the gift of the Holy

Ghost. For the promise is unto you, and to your children, and to all that are afar off, even as many as the Lord our God shall call." Peter told them to repent. Translated in the Greek "repent" is the word metanoeo (met-an-o-eh-o), which means to think differently, or afterwards, that is to reconsider, morally to feel guilt. This word is important because repentance is the obedience part to receive the promise of the Holy Spirit. The people responded to the word spoken and accepted the promised blessing of Abraham. Three thousand souls joined the faith, but that was not the end. God had a plan for all mankind to be saved, it not only happened for them, but this same blessing would pour out on the Gentiles. Galatians 3:14 says, "That the blessing of Abraham might come on the Gentiles through Jesus Christ; that we might receive the promise of the Spirit through faith." I like this verse because of the word receive; the word receive translated in the Greek is lambano (Strong's #G2983). It means to gain, get, obtain, but let me share the definition the Lord gave me. He said, "This word receive means to take possession of the person," to take us as one's own, His own. This is not saying that we take possession, it is saying He takes you, He takes us, He takes over us as the possession. He catches us. He gains us. He seizes us. He accepts us through faith. It is the faith that snatches us.

Blessing here in Galatians 3:14 is translated in the Greek as eulogia (Strong's #2129), which means "fine speaking, that is, elegance of language." Eulogia comes from a Greek word eulogeo meaning to speak well of, praise, prosper. The breakdown of eulogeo comes from two Greek words Eu: good, well (done), and logos: something said through thought, reasoning, word, a divine expression that is Christ. Therefore, God in Genesis 12:1-3, God told Abraham that the blessing was going to happen through the announcement or speaking well of the good news of Jesus Christ and that God would pour out His Spirit upon all flesh through Jesus, God's seed, through faith (believing that Jesus is the Messiah/Anointed One through whom we will obtain eternal salvation). God's intentions were to give a full life of wholeness and abundance. This will happen and all people will know, even if they don't believe or receive His promise. Romans 16:26 says, "Now, however, that truth has been brought out into the open through the writings of the prophets; and by the command of the eternal God it is made known to all nations, so that all may believe an obey" (Good News Bible).

What's so exciting is that we are promised the Holy Spirit and without Him we cannot obey. We need Him to help us to keep God's Word and to lead us to righteousness. Ezekiel 36:27 says, "I will put My Spirit within you and cause you to walk in My statutes, and you will keep My judgments and do them." Oh boy, talk about being fully possessed by the Holy Spirit causing the believers to live from the inside out. What a great way to live holy before Jesus. Galatians 5:16 is another interesting scripture, "Walk in the Spirit, and you shall not fulfill the lust of the flesh." In other words, live from the inside out, allowing the Holy Spirit to control every part of you, being humbly dependent on Him for everything, trusting Him through it all.

To unlock everything in the Holy Spirit is to receive the Spirit through obedience because it unlocks all the spiritual and physical benefits in him for the believer. Did you know that the blessing comes in two forms: concrete (physical) and abstract (spiritual)? The blessing in concrete form is described in Deuteronomy 28:3-14:

"Blessed shalt thou be in the city, and blessed shalt thou be in the field. (This represents the commerce, trade and agriculture), Blessed shall be the fruit of thy body, and the fruit of thy ground, and the fruit of thy cattle, the increase of thy kine, and the flocks of thy sheep. (This represents fertility and economic prosperity), Blessed shall be thy basket and thy store (this represents food supply). Blessed shalt thou be when thou comest in, and blessed shalt thou be when thou goest out. The Lord shall cause thine enemies that rise up against thee to be smitten before thy face: they shall come out against thee one way, and flee before thee seven ways. The Lord shall command the blessing upon thee in thy storehouses, and in all that thou settest thine hand unto; and he shall bless thee in the land which the Lord thy God giveth thee. The Lord shall establish thee an holy people unto himself, as he hath sworn unto thee, if thou shalt keep the commandments of the Lord thy God, and walk in his ways. And all people of the earth shall see that thou art called by the name of the Lord; and they shall be afraid of thee. And the Lord shall make thee plenteous in goods, in the fruit of thy body, and in the fruit of thy cattle, and in the fruit of thy ground, in the land which the Lord sware unto thy fathers to give thee. The Lord shall open unto thee his good treasure, the heaven to give the rain unto thy land in his season, and to bless all the work of thine hand: and thou shalt lend unto many nations, and thou shalt not borrow. And the Lord shall make thee the head, and not the tail; and thou shalt be above only, and thou shalt not be beneath; (This represents being leaders and not followers) if that thou hearken unto the commandments of the Lord thy God, which I command thee this day, to observe and to do them."

The blessing in abstract (spiritual) form is described in Ephesians 1:3-14:

"Blessed be the God and Father of our Lord Jesus Christ, who hath blessed us with all spiritual blessings in heavenly places in Christ: According as he hath chosen us in him before the foundation of the world, that we should be holy and without blame before him in love: Having predestined us unto the adoption of children by Jesus Christ to himself, according to the good pleasure of his will, To the praise of the glory of his grace, wherein he hath made us accepted in the beloved. In whom we have redemption through his blood, the forgiveness of sins, according to the riches of his grace; Wherein he hath abounded toward us in all wisdom and prudence; Having made known unto us the mystery of his will, according to his good pleasure which he hath purposed in himself: That in the dispensation of the fulness of times he might gather together in one all things in Christ, both which are in heaven, and which are on earth; even in him: In whom also we have obtained an inheritance, being predestined according to the purpose of him who worketh all things after the counsel of his own will: That we should be to the praise of his glory, who first trusted in Christ. In whom ye also trusted, after that ye heard the word of truth, the gospel of your salvation: in whom also after that ye believed, ye were sealed with that holy Spirit of promise, Which is the earnest of our inheritance until the redemption of the purchased possession, unto the praise of his glory."

Believers (the body of Christ) have the physical and spiritual blessings of Jesus. Now we understand that the blessing is the Holy Spirit of Jesus Christ and He has no limitations. We can have Him in full.

CHAPTER NINE
THE FULLNESS OF THE BLESSING

שמע

L et's go back to the beginning of the fall of man. God gave Adam an order: that he could liberally eat from every tree in the Garden of Eden except the tree of the knowledge of good and evil. Eating from that tree would cause him to die (live apart from God, physical death). Then God made Adam a wife from Adam's rib and Adam called her woman (Genesis 2:16-17, 21-23). In the garden there was a serpent who was more cunning than any other beast of the field. He starting talking to the woman. He didn't introduce himself. He didn't ask how she was doing. He simply asked her this question, "Did God really say, 'You must not eat from any tree in the garden?'"

She answered the serpent and said, "We may eat fruit from the trees in the garden, but God did say, You must not eat fruit from the tree that is in the middle of the garden, and you must not touch it or you will die.'"

The serpent lied to her and said, "You will not die." So she ate from the tree of the knowledge of good and evil and gave a piece to Adam as well. Then Adam and the woman heard God walking in the garden and they hid from Him.

God called for Adam, "Where are you?"

Adam told God, "I was hiding because I am naked."

God said, "Who told you; you were naked and did you eat from the tree that I ordered you not to eat?" Adam blamed the woman and God asked her what she did. She blamed the serpent. God disciplined all three parties (Genesis 3:14-19), but God said something specific to the serpent in Genesis 3:15, "And I will put enmity between thee and the woman, and between thy seed and her seed; it shall bruise thy head, and thou shalt bruise his heel" (KJV). The Lord showed me an image of this verse: Jesus crushed Satan's head and it made him dysfunctional, so everything about Satan is dysfunctional. Genesis 3:15 is the first prophecy about Jesus and the first gospel message of the promised blessing, which is Jesus. What is the fullness of the blessing? He is the Holy Spirit…without limits, the blessing of Christ (the anointed one). The fullness of the blessing came on Jesus; we can read about this in the New Testament:

Matthew 3:16

"And Jesus, when he was baptized, went up straightway out of the water: and, lo, the heavens were opened unto him, and he saw the Spirit of God (Holy Spirit) descending like a dove, and lighting (power) upon him."

Matthew 12:18

"Behold my servant, whom I have chosen; my beloved, in whom my soul is well pleased: I will put my spirit upon him, and he shall shew judgment to the Gentiles."

Luke 4:18-19
"The Spirit of the Lord is upon me, because he hath
anointed me to preach the gospel to the poor; he hath
sent me to heal the brokenhearted, to preach deliverance
to the captives, and recovering of sight to the blind,
to set at liberty them that are bruised, To preach the
acceptable year of the Lord."

What do these verses mean? In Acts 10:38 Peter explains, "God anointed Jesus of Nazareth with the Holy Ghost and with power: who went about doing good, and healing all that were oppressed of the devil; for God was with him." The fullness of the blessing came on Jesus and overtook Him to be the blessing so that whoever received Jesus would have the same measure in Christ.

Operating in the fullness of the blessing means allowing the full control of the power of the Holy Spirit of Christ to operate in you. It means humbling yourself under the full control of the power of the Holy Spirit of Christ which activates or ignites the gift (power) of His fullness in you. When the fullness of the blessing comes, you become a servant or slave of the Spirit for His purpose, permitting yourself to go through the process of Christ's will. When we make Jesus Christ our Lord, He becomes our master through His Holy Spirit. We (believers) learn to obey him through allowing ourselves to be used by him. First Corinthians 6:19-20 (AMP) says, "Do you not know that your body is a temple of the Holy Spirit who is within (with you and in you), whom you have received as a gift from Jesus, and that you are not your own [property]?" Jesus bought and paid a heavy price for you and now the Holy Spirit of Christ lives in you so that you can do a specific function for the kingdom of God. Here is an example: when a company hires someone for a job, there is a cost to recruit, cost for salary, and cost for training. When the company hires, they expect for a person to comply with their specific functions, rules, policies, and instructions. If you were hired by a company, by law you have to obey because the owner hired you and is paying you to do a job; you cannot just do whatever you want. If you do, then there will be consequences to your actions. Therefore, remember Jesus paid a price, He exchanged His life for yours. In Christ there are rules, specific functions, policies, and instructions, because God is holy (set apart) so that means you are set apart to do a specific function and God expects for you to do it. When we as believers, "the children of God," step outside His purpose, there are consequences. Having the fullness of the blessing gives believers purpose. Dictionary.com defines purpose as "the reason for which something exists or is done, made, and used; an intended or desired result, end, aim, goal, and determination." I've wondered why we sometimes get out of His proposed plan since God has a strategic plan or purpose for our lives. One reason is because we don't understand our purpose, and another reason is that we often don't think we're worthy of the places God wants to take us. We question him like, "Wait a minute. This doesn't feel right or sound right. This can't be real...this can't be happening to me." However, the Lord has a strategic purpose and plan for each one of our lives and one of the main components of how you know you are walking in your purpose is whenever you step out in your purpose, you encounter what I call "little fireworks" that come to distract you.

While you're living out the purpose through obedience because of the fullness of the blessing of Christ, instructions will come and obstacles will arise as you listen to instructions. Psalm 23:1 reassures us that the Lord is our Shepherd, and in verse four, it also says, "Yea though I walk through the valley of the shadow of death, I will fear no evil: for thou art with me." As you walk in purpose, be reminded that His power, authority, protection, and care are with you. When David wrote this he knew there was a purpose for his life. As he walked in his purpose even prior to him becoming a king, there were different obstacles. David was able to go through the process, become a great king, and continue walking in his kingship even during the craziest and most trying times. There were many instances when King Saul was threatening David's life, but the Bible says that, "David behaved wisely in all his ways; and the Lord was with him and when Saul saw that David was successful and prosperous he became afraid of David because the Lord was with him." (1 Samuel 18:14). We have two important words in this verse: which are behaved and wisely. Behaved is defined by the Webster Dictionary of 1828 as "to conduct (oneself) in proper manner, to manage the actions of (oneself) in a particular way." The second word wisely describes how David behaved. Wisely, translated in Hebrew is the word sakal (saw-kal). It means the ability to consider a situation with comprehension in order to be successful or prosperous (Ancient Hebrew Lexicon #7919). In other words, David had the ability to act intelligently towards King Saul and his threats and he successfully advanced in everything Saul gave him to do.

Although Saul continuously tried to set David up to fail, the Lord was with David and gave him the wisdom on how to succeed in every area that King Saul tried to make David look like a failure. This is a lesson for you and I. When you're in your purpose, remember the Lord is with you and He will give you the wisdom to advance and succeed. Just as when obstacles or people who are being led by evil spirits come after you or try to set you up for failure, understand that the Lord is with you while you are in your purpose. Even though you are in the valley of the shadow of death, Psalm 23 reminds us that the Lord is with you while you are in your purpose. The Lord has given you the mind of Christ with understanding and wisdom to finish your course to get through every situation. This is why Psalm 23:5 says, "You prepare a table before me in the presence of my enemies." God has already made a way for you to prosper and advance and He will do it in your enemies' faces.

When something seems strange or when a person is behaving negatively towards you and it's unexplainable and out of order, remember this: Satan is behind it. He is there because you became an obedient Christian as a result of the fullness of the blessing of Christ. Many people get dismantled or confused during these trying times. They ask God, "Why did this happen?" Others get upset while the Lord is like, "No, keep going my way and don't forget I've given you authority." There are obstacles (situations and people) that will try to interrupt your obedient life, and instead of asking, "Why is this person interrupting my life?" you can take authority. Most of the time, in order for you to receive an answer to this question, you will have to pray and ask the Father. He will give you the answer and wisdom for the situation, and even if He doesn't give an answer, He can use the situation to build your listening and hearing skills and mature your character and understanding of the anointing of the blessing of Christ. If you really think about it, these situations produce obedience in you. A lot of the called-out ones who are filled with the blessing don't fully understand. Here is an example the Lord gave me about a guy I knew five years ago. He said, "His purpose is to be a father, a husband, and teach his children my word, but when his wife comes up against him he begins to ask me questions like, 'Why is it that every time I want to be a good husband, good father, and teach my children your word, my wife interrupts me?'" God said, "I give the answer all the time, but he doesn't listen. I say to him, 'No, just let her do it; you keep doing what I tell you to do because this is your purpose.'" And the Lord said the man would reply to him, "No this is not my purpose. I'm supposed to do this," and the Lord answered back saying, "No get back in my will; this what you were born to do. This is what I called you for. This is what you are supposed to do."

Then the Lord started talking to me about His church (His body of believers). He said, "My children don't [understand what happens] when they are walking in their purpose because of the fullness of the blessing of Christ through obedience. They don't understand that it's normal when interruptions come. Being rebellious, they say, 'No, this is not what I want to do because it's uncomfortable.'" The Lord said, "Of course it's going to be uncomfortable because you don't know your purpose and because all your life you have been going a certain way, and now I'm actually placing you in your purpose, in the area you were born for which you have never walked in until this day. And the person would say again, 'No, I'm not doing that.'" And the Lord says, "What do you mean; this is what I called you for, this is why you are in the earth. You have to live out your purpose, you don't understand because all your life you have walked in your own purpose, but now you are awake to my will. As long as you are rebellious and keep thinking to yourself that you want to do what you want to do, then there will always be some type of pushback, because you are out of my purpose. You don't understand now, but keep walking with me, and you will get the full understanding, as you are walking. I will give you the directions, the wisdom, and the understanding. I will give you all the know-how during your walk in purpose because of the fullness of the blessing of Christ which is leading you in obedience." Then the Lord began to talk about how the Bible speaks about when we are born again, we are a new creation. Believers become something they were not before and the Lord says, "Don't fight against it. Just walk with me. I'm directing your path. As you are going through the purpose, try to not ask so many questions, because the answer is: you are walking in your purpose." Then He says, "A lot of people don't know what their purpose is. For instance, a lot of women are called to be mothers, and I have placed children in their wombs, and a lot of women say, "No, I don't want to be a mother. I just want to drink and smoke and I still want to party." The Lord says, "No, I gave you these children for a purpose and I need you to listen to me so I can teach you how to raise these children because later on in life, these children have a purpose."

The Lord again spoke about the crazy things that come while we are in our purpose because of the fullness of the blessing. He said, "Combative things come because you are in your purpose. For instance, have you ever thought, 'Oh! that's weird or that person is weird towards you?' It's weird because when they see you, they see me, and you are actually walking in my purpose, my will. Of course you're going to look weird, but you're not weird or abnormal, it's just that you are acting on my purpose."

God said to me, "I told Moses to speak to Pharaoh and tell him 'this is what I'm going to do.' Sometimes Moses did not understand his purpose, but he knew he was my prophet. He knew he was my servant, and he knew he had to carry my people across to the promised land. However, he saw the promised land but didn't go in because of disobedience." The Lord said, "My son Jesus knew what His purpose one hundred percent that's why He has always said, 'I am here to do the will of my father and when Jesus was walking in

His purpose, a lot of things came up against Him, but He did not take it personally because He knew what He was born to this earth to do." We can find Jesus' purposes in a number of places in the Bible, but just to give you one that most people know it is in Luke 4:18-19.

"The Spirit of the Lord is on me, because he has anointed me to proclaim good news to the poor. He has sent me to proclaim freedom for the prisoners and recovery of sight for the blind, to set the oppressed free, to proclaim the year of the Lord's favor" (NIV).

The Lord had more to say to me. He continued, "So when my people are walking in my purpose it's not about the agitation or people against them. When stuff comes up, they need an understanding that they are walking in my purpose."

I know that this was a lot that the Lord had to say, however we all needed to hear this because as He said, "Most will not receive the fullness of the blessing because they will not accept my word which gives my purpose."

He said, "It was not hard for Jesus because He received His purpose," then He took me to the place where Jesus said in John 6:38, "For I have come down from heaven, not to do My own will, but to do the will of Him who sent me" (AMP). So I ask a question: Why don't some receive the purpose of the fullness of Christ? Now remember the Lord said before because they will not accept His Word. Jesus explained in Mark 4:13-19:

> "The sower soweth the word. And these are they by the wayside, where the word is sown; but when they have heard, Satan cometh immediately, and taketh away the word that was sown in their hearts. And these are they likewise which are sown on stony ground; who, when they have heard the word, immediately receive it with gladness; And have no

root in themselves, and so endure but for a time: afterward, when affliction or persecution ariseth for the word's sake, immediately they are offended. And these are they which are sown among thorns; such as hear the word, And the cares of this world, and the deceitfulness of riches, and the lusts of other things entering in, choke the word, and it becometh unfruitful."

People don't receive the fullness of the blessing of Christ because after God speaks His Word, Satan comes immediately because they are not paying attention. Some have no root—nothing to hold on to, because of pressures, mistreatments, and hostility, traps, offenses, distractions, delusions of wealth and possessions, and longing or craving empty things. However, if the person can just accept God's Word as is and act on it with obedience, no matter what, then it will produce fruit without measure. So as you can see, the fullness of the blessing has a purpose and receiving the fullness of the blessing requires obedience.

Philippians 4:13 says, "I can do all things through Christ which strengthens me." It is through Christ the anointed one who gives us strength to do everything that the fullness of the blessing purposely instructs and guides the believer to do. When you're full of the blessing of Christ for His purpose, you are supplied and equipped to do His work. Philippians 14:19 says, "But my God shall supply all your need according to His riches in glory by Christ Jesus." Paul prayed for the church of Philippi that they too will be full of the blessing for every need and business affairs in their lives to empower them to prosper spiritually and materially, that Jesus will make full, to fill up, to cause to abound. In other words, Jesus gives the fullness of the blessing without limits or measure. In John

3:34 (AMP) it says, "For He whom God has sent speaks the words of God [proclaiming the Father's own message]; for God gives the [gift of the] Spirit without measure [generously and boundlessly]!" Since believers are carrying the fullness, we can do all things that are purposely given to us to do from God and we are given this fullness without measure so that makes us well equipped for His good work even if there is interruption or trouble. Born again believers have the fullness of the blessing of the gospel of Christ. All we have to do is obey His voice.

THE KEY TO THE BLESSING

CHAPTER TEN
OBEY MY VOICE

שמע

J esus said, "If you love me keep my commandments." How can we keep His commandments? The answer is by obeying the voice of the Holy Spirit. The physician Luke wrote the gospel of Luke and the book of Acts. Acts is a continuation of His gospel and the purpose was to share all that Jesus did and to demonstrate to His gentile-based audience that Jesus is indeed the Christ. Luke's main concern in the book of Acts was to show how the gospel spread from a Jerusalem, Jewish-centered sect of Judaism to a global, Gentile-based movement. We learn that this was possible due to the Holy Spirit.

In Acts 1:1-4, Luke is sharing with Theophilus the teachings Jesus conducted through the Holy Spirit until He was taken up. We learn in verses three and four that when Jesus was alive after the resurrection He began to speak to His disciples and commanded for them to remain in Jerusalem until they received the promise of the father. Jesus commanded them to wait in a place (Jerusalem), then Jesus told them why they needed to wait. "Ye have heard of me, for John truly baptized with water but ye shall be baptized with the Holy Spirit not many days" (Acts 1:4-5 KJV). He also told them,

"But ye shall receive power, after that the Holy Ghost is come upon you: and ye shall be witnesses unto me both in Jerusalem, and in all Judaea, and in Samaria, and unto the uttermost part of the earth" (Acts 1:8 KJV).

Now let's take a look at these words so you can see how obeying the voice is important. The Bible says that Jesus "commanded" the disciples to wait (verse four). The word command translated in the Greek is parangellō (par-ang-gel-lo) from para, which means "from close-beside" and aggello, which means "inform" properly, to charge, to transmit a message, give a command that is **fully authorized** because it has gone through all the proper (necessary) channels. Jesus commands (paraggello) believers to act as He **authorizes** them through the revelation of faith (His inward persuasions). This word command is also used as a military term, and you have to understand that Jesus is the Commander in Chief and He knew the exact place where the Holy Spirit, the power of God was going to be. He gave the official charge for the disciples to stay in Jerusalem, which was where and why they had to wait. The word "wait" translated in the Greek from Strong's Concordance #G4037 is perimeno (per-ee-men-o), peri means around; meno means to stay in a given place, remain, abide, continue, dwell, endure, be present, stand, and tarry. In other words, it means to remain all-around steady regardless of obstacles. Here is the picture the Lord gave me about command and wait. He said, "Think of this as being in the military and I'm the commander in chief who knows the right spot to attack to have victory. Even though the place and time does not make sense because of what's going on around you, just obey my voice then at that moment, at the right time, you will receive victory—what I want to give you. This is why command and faith is so connected."

Now after Jesus commanded the disciples to remain, they experienced just what Jesus said they would—they received power when the Holy Spirit came upon them. This happened because the apostles obeyed His voice. Read Acts 1:12-14 when you have a moment. Due to their obedience, something amazing happened in Acts 2:1-18. The Bible says, "And when the day of Pentecost was fully come, they were all with one accord in one place. And suddenly there came a sound from heaven as of a rushing mighty wind, and it filled all the house, where they were sitting. And there appeared unto them cloven tongues like as of fire, and it sat upon each of them. And they were all filled with the Holy Ghost, and began to speak with other tongues, as the Spirit gave them utterance." Now while all of this was going on, different types of people that were from other regions far from Jerusalem who spoke different languages heard the disciples speaking their language after the fullness of the Holy Spirit came on the disciples. This all happened because they obeyed the voice of Jesus and with their obedience, power in the fullness of the Spirit (or the force of the blessing of Jesus) came on them. Now, can you see what it really means to obey the voice of our Lord? He gave the fullness of the blessing so that you and I can speak and live out the blessing for others to receive.

So after everyone heard the disciples speak in their own native language, the crowd of different people began to wonder if they were drunk but as we know the disciples were not; they were filled with the Holy Spirit of Christ, who was speaking through them. Again because the Apostles obeyed the voice of the Lord another amazing thing happened. On the day of Pentecost when the people **heard** the disciples speak the blessing of the promise of the Holy Spirit, which was spoken by the Prophet Joel, and after hearing Peter explain what was said, the crowds of people obeyed through repentance and received the fullness of the blessing of the promise.

Acts 2:14-17 says:

"But Peter, standing up with the eleven, lifted up his voice, and said unto them, Ye men of Judaea, and all ye that dwell at Jerusalem, be this known unto you, and hearken to my words: For these are not drunken, as ye suppose, seeing it is but the third hour of the day. But this is that which was spoken by the prophet Joel; And it shall come to pass in the last days, saith God , I will pour out of my Spirit upon all flesh: and your sons and your daughters shall prophesy, and your young men shall see visions, and your old men shall dream dreams."

Peter continued in Acts 2:22-36:

"Ye men of Israel, hear these words; Jesus of Nazareth, a man approved of God among you by miracles and wonders and signs, which God did by him in the midst of you, as ye yourselves also know: Him, being delivered by the determinate counsel and foreknowledge of God, ye have taken, and by wicked hands have crucified and slain: Whom God hath raised up, having loosed the pains of death: because it was not possible that he should be holden of it. For David speaketh concerning him, I foresaw the Lord always before my face, for he is on my right hand, that I should not be moved: Therefore did my heart rejoice, and my tongue was glad; moreover also my flesh shall rest in hope: Because thou wilt not leave my soul in hell, neither wilt thou suffer thine Holy One to see corruption. Thou hast made known to me the ways of life; thou shalt make me full of joy with thy countenance then Peter said, "Men and brethren, let me freely speak unto you of the patriarch David, that he is both dead and buried, and his sepulcher (is with us unto this da. Therefore being a prophet, and knowing that God had sworn with an oath to him, that of the fruit of his loins, according to the flesh, he would raise up Christ to sit on his throne; He seeing this before spake of the resurrection of Christ, that his soul was not left in hell, neither his flesh did see corruption. This Jesus hath God raised up, whereof we all are witnesses. Therefore being by the right hand of God exalted, and having received of the Father the promise of the Holy Ghost, he hath shed forth this, which ye now see and hear. For David is not ascended into the heavens: but he saith himself, The Lord said unto my Lord, Sit thou on my right hand, Until I make thy foes thy footstool. Therefore let all the house of Israel know assuredly, that God hath made the same Jesus, whom ye have crucified, both Lord and Christ."

Acts 2:37-41 continues:

"Now when they <u>heard</u> this, they were pricked in their heart, **and said unto Peter and to the rest of the apostles, Men and brethren, what shall we do?** Then Peter said unto them, Repent, and be baptized every one of you in the name of Jesus Christ for the remission of sins, and ye shall receive the gift of the Holy Ghost. For the promise is unto you, and to your children, and to all that are afar off, even as many as the Lord our God shall call."

Verse 37 in bold above really made me read it twice, because the people said, "What shall we do?" This is interesting! The crowd of people that were all different heard Peter preach about Jesus then asked "what shall we do?" I want you to understand this: the people

<u>heard.</u> Heard defined from the Merriam-Webster Dictionary means to perceive or become aware of by the ear, to gain knowledge, to listen to with attention. So they obeyed through hearing, meaning they paid attention to the words with understanding and responded with action, the multitude of people literally heard and took action. We can see this in Acts 2:41-47 (Read it when you have a chance.). Romans 10:14-16 literally tells us one has to hear. Paul wrote:

> "How then shall they call on him in whom they have not believed? and how shall they believe in him of whom they have not heard? and how shall they hear without a preacher? And how shall they preach, except they be sent? as it is written, How beautiful are the feet of them that preach the gospel of peace, and bring glad tidings of good things! But they have not all obeyed the gospel. For Esaias saith, Lord, who hath believed our report? So then faith cometh by hearing, and hearing by the word of God."

Here is a quote from Aaron Lynch (Co-founder of Path of Obedience, www.pathofobedience.com) published on July 29, 2016: "The action of obedience is our only sure measure of successful listening."

Let's discuss the voice we are supposed to obey. In the Bible we have a letter written to Hebrew Christians. It was written because they were suffering from persecution of standing firm in their faith in Jesus Christ. They were experiencing pressure, they began to waiver, and they were tempted to go back to their old ways of Judaism. Hebrews 1:1 says, "Jesus who at sundry (many times) and in divers manners (many ways) spake in time past unto the fathers by the Prophets, (Old Testament). Hath in these last days spoken unto us **by His Son,** whom he hath appointed heir of all things, by whom also he made the worlds." Verse two tells us who is speaking to us today, that is the Son of God, Jesus. Then the Word goes on to say in Hebrews 2:1, "Therefore we ought to give the more earnest heed to the things which we have heard, lest at any time we should let them slip." What are the previous things that were spoken, which require our attention? Before I get to the answer, let me share what the Lord wants you to know first. He dealt with me about paying more attention to His Word. I was in my bed still sleeping and the voice of the Lord woke me up and began to say, "Receive my word."

I said, "How do I receive your word?"

The Spirit of the Lord said, "Don't think about it, just do. The problem is believers think about what I say, when they should do what I say. Take for instance Eve and the serpent in Genesis 3:1 where the serpent said to Eve, 'Yea hath God, said, ye shall not eat of every tree of the garden.' The serpent gave Eve something to think about when all she had to do is do what I said to do, which was not to eat."

I said to the Lord, "How do I not think, but do?"

He answered, "Don't think, know I am God." Then He gave me Psalm 46:10 which says, "Be still and know that I am God." Then He explained this text. He said, "This means stop thinking and know I am God." The reason why the Spirit of Lord wanted me to place this here is that I had a situation that was crazy, and I communicated to the Lord in prayer about the situation which was about some neighbors living right next door who were harassing and causing me trouble. I was trying to figure out how God was going to make them flee, however the Lord had already told me what He was going to do, so I took this as Him checking me to get it together and pay attention to His Word, so I stopped thinking and began to meditate on the fact that He is God.

Now back to the answer to the question. Who do we give the more earnest heed to/pay attention to? Hebrews 12:24-25 gives us the answer. It says, "And to **Jesus** the mediator of the new covenant, and to the blood of sprinkling, that speaks better things than that of Abel. See that ye refuse not him (Christ Jesus) that speaks. For if they (this refers to the children of Israel the first generation) escaped not who refused him (The voice of the Lord) that spake on earth, much more shall not we (believers) escape, if we turn away from him (Christ Jesus who is at the right hand of God, the Word) that speaketh from heaven." These verses tell us that Christ Jesus is speaking to us today through His Holy Spirit.

Now I want you, the reader, to listen, see, and understand. Hebrews 3:15 (NLT) says this, "Remember what it says: Today when you hear His voice, don't harden your hearts as Israel did when they rebelled." As a believer in Christ when you hear His voice NOW, TODAY, do not turn your ear and refuse to listen to him. Let me give you something to think about. When we say "Christ," we are speaking of the Anointed One. Christ is the voice to obey. He is the Holy Spirit. He is the Spirit of Truth, the Comforter who speaks. Here are a few texts that give us proof He is the voice to obey.

Philippians 1:19
"For I know that this shall turn to my salvation through your prayer, and the supply of the Spirit of Jesus Christ…"

2 Corinthians 3:17 (AMP)
"Now the Lord is the Spirit, and where the Spirit of the Lord is, there is liberty [emancipation from bondage, true freedom]."

The Holy Spirit is a general title of the Spirit of God. The Spirit of God is a particular expression and refers to the Spirit of the incarnate savior who is Jesus. John 7:37 (AMP) says:

"Now on the last and most important day of the feast, Jesus stood and called out [in a loud voice], 'If anyone is thirsty, let him come to Me and drink! He who believes in Me [who adheres to, trusts in, and relies on Me], as the Scripture has said, 'From his innermost being will flow continually rivers of living water. But He was speaking of the [Holy] Spirit, whom those who believed in Him [as Savior] were to receive afterward. The Spirit had not yet been given, because Jesus was not yet glorified (raised to honor).'"

The Comforter, Jesus, was referring to the Holy Spirit, His inner voice, His Spirit, which would be in the believer and on the believer. Christ, the Anointed One, is different in title and functions than the Holy Spirit, but is one with Him.

In conclusion, I pray that you will obey His voice now and receive the fullness of the blessing so that you may be blessed by Him, who has the blessing, who is Jesus. The ways to live out your blessing are to love through obedience, be obedient to the faith so that you will be prosperous and have success, and live righteously by the Word of God. Listening and hearing with understanding and having the faith to believe like Abraham through obedience. I pray that you receive this teaching and message from the heart of the Father. Glory be to the Father and the Lord, Jesus Christ, amen.

About the Author

Crystal Noel Wyatt (Ambassador Wyatt) is a believer of Jesus Christ who is called by God to teach His people. Her specific assignment is to help believers fulfill God's calling through an understanding of obedience, love, and faith. As an author and teacher, Ambassador Wyatt writes and teaches by divine revelation, wisdom, and knowledge.

She has been married for sixteen years, and is a mother to one son. Ambassador Wyatt graduated from the Pistis School of Ministry in Southfield, Michigan. She holds an Associate of Applied Science degree in Health Science from Brown Mackie College in Cincinnati, Ohio and a Diploma in Licensed Practical Nursing from the same school. She is a retired nurse and president of Ambassador Wyatt Christian Collection.

Ambassador Wyatt enjoys designing, writing, singing, teaching the Word of God and spending time at the beach enjoying life and God's creations.

www.ingramcontent.com/pod-product-compliance
Lightning Source LLC
Chambersburg PA
CBHW071150090426
42736CB00012B/2291